LURKING DOUBT

Other Books by
Glenn Alan Cheney

Quilombo dos Palmares:
Brazil's Lost Nation of Fugitive Slaves

Thanksgiving: The Pilgrims' First Year in America

Journey on the Estrada Real:
Encounters in the Mountains of Brazil

Love and Death in the Kingdom of Swaziland

His Hands on Earth: Courage, Compassion, Charism,
and the Missionary Sisters of the Sacred Heart of Jesus

How a Nation Grieves: Press Accounts of the Death of Lincoln,
the Hunt for Booth, and America in Mourning

The Merry Burial Compendium

Dr. Jamoke's Little Book of Hitherto Uncompiled
Facts and Curiosities Regarding Bees

The Cat Caboodle: A Litter Box of Cat Facts and Curiosities

Be Revolutionary: Some Thoughts from Pope Francis

Frankenstein on the Cusp of Something

Law of the Jungle: Environmental Anarchy
and the Tenharim People of Amazonia

More titles at NLLibrarium.com

LURKING DOUBT

NOTES ON
INCARCERATION

Glenn Alan Cheney

New London Librarium

Lurking Doubt: Notes on Incarceration
by Glenn Alan Cheney

Cover art by Glenn Cheney

Copyright © 2018 Glenn Alan Cheney

Published by
New London Librarium
Hanover, CT 06350
NLLibrarium.com

ISBNs
Hardcover: 978-1-947074-17-0
Paperback: 978-1-947074-15-6
eBook: 978-1-947074-16-3

Printed in the United States

...the Court must in the end ask itself a subjective question,
whether we are content to let the matter stand as it is,
or whether there is not some lurking doubt in our minds
which makes us wonder whether an injustice has been done.

JOHN PASSMORE WIDGERY
LORD CHIEF JUSTICE OF ENGLAND AND WALES

Contents

Introduction

This book does not purport or pretend to be a thorough examination of the history or current state of imprisonment. It touches all too lightly, too briefly, on only a few of imprisonment's many serious problems. Its only purpose is to give the reader a sampling of the information that is available.

A lot of information is available. Innumerable studies identify innumerable problems with the current use of prisons as a form of punishment and personal improvement. Recidivism rates indicate clearly and undeniably that imprisonment fails to make society safer. As a deterrent, prisons are minimally, if indeterminately, effective. As a form of mandatory "correction," they fail miserably. They aggravate violence, destroy families, drain public funds, cause poverty, hurt children, and accomplish little more than temporarily isolating a criminal from society and giving a few people the satisfaction of revenge.

Some of those innumerable studies explore solutions. Some are just ideas, others actual programs proven to work. Shorter sentences, fewer sentences, more family visits, working with animals, religious conversion, art programs, college courses, meditation, shorter and less demanding paroles, more responsibility, restorative justice, less youth incarceration, even doing away with prisons altogether—there is so much that could be done, yet social, political, and economic pressures too often prevent change. The ever-popular "tough on crime" approach rarely recognizes the possibility that inducing a former criminal to go straight is more productive than making a criminal suffer. This book is one in a series of short books with brief narratives on a given subject.

The first books, however, were of a different nature. One looked at little known facts about bees. Another examined death and burial from unusual perspectives. Another took a light-hearted look at cats. They were all a bit frivolous, if a bit technical, meant to entertain as much as inform the reader. But the research into prisons, prisoners, and imprisonment quickly became too dark to treat so flippantly. Prisons are a real problem, a sad, painful, tragedy affecting, at the moment, over two million people in the United States, with millions more in the pipeline of racism, poverty, and erosion of generally accepted social values. The gravity of the problem and the existence of solutions led to a book that is distinct in the series.

In that each topic in this book is presented in just a few paragraphs, the author hopes that interested reader will refer to the documents cited in footnotes.

Many of these references are available on web sites, and they tend to have footnotes of their own, tempting the reader from casual reading into deeper research.

But neither reading nor research is enough. Something—a lot of things—need to be done. Solutions exist. They are known. What is not known is why the solutions are enacted only sporadically, if at all.

Prison Life

Meet & Greet

Welcome to your new home! It may not be as spacious as you like, but at least you'll have someone to talk to.

You may not be escorted to your cell. A guard will give you a cell number and point the way. If you can't find your cell, find someone who looks like you and ask where to go.

The first thing you have to do is meet your new roomie. This will be a big moment for both of you, and perhaps a bit awkward. The thing to do upon arrival is knock on the door. If there's someone inside, introduce yourself thus: "My name's Bob. They told me to bunk here."

If no one's there, go in, but don't touch anything. Don't lie on a bunk. Just wait. Stand up to introduce yourself.

Your cell mate may need some time to clean off the bunk that will be yours. It's a good time to break a little ice. Ask for advice. Where do I put my stuff? When do we eat? What's the rule on leaving and coming back? Don't ask any personal questions. Presume the best. Be nice—polite but not weak.

Glenn Alan Cheney

Read Up to Survive

Know someone going to prison? There are books on how to go about being a prisoner and surviving imprisonment. Some titles:

Behind Bars: Surviving Prison, Jeffrey Ian Ross, Alpha, 2002.

Prison Survival Guide: Words of Wisdom and Encouragement from an Inmate, Russell Ferguson, Rosedog Books, 2016.

How to Do Time: What to Expect and How to Survive When Going to Prison, Jamonz M. Ross and Taleana K. Ross, 2017.

How to Survive in Prison: A Guide for Prisoners, their Families and Supporters, Createspace, 2017.

How to Survive Prison for the First Time Inmate: Take a Look at a Dangerous Society within our Society, Createspace, 2009.

How to Survive Prison, Andrew V. Kudin, Amazon Digital, 2012.

First Timers Guide on How to Survive in New York State Prison, Kemp McCoy, Trafford, 2013.

Inmate to Convict: A Guide to Prison Survival and the Art of Penitentiary Warfare, Brian Anderson, Amazon Digital, 2016.

Federal Prison Handbook: the Definitive Guide to Surviving the Federal Bureau of Prison, Christopher Zoukis, Middle St. Pub. 2017.

Any Questions?

Federal Prison: A Comprehensive Survival Guide, by Jonathan Richards (out of print) purports to answer these questions:

> Will I be assaulted? What will the other inmates think of me? Will I be extorted? Will I be strip-searched? Will I be given a body cavity search? What will a normal day be like? How will I pass the time? Will I be able to exercise? What will I eat?   Will I be locked in a cell? What will the sleeping arrangements be like? Will I have to shower in front of other men? Will I have to go to the bathroom in front of other men? Can I bring anything with me? Which one of the hundreds of federal prisons out there will I be sent to? What about my medications? Will I be locked up with murderers and rapists? What if I get sick? Will everyone know the details of my crime? What will happen to my business? How soon and how often can I have visitors? What will the prison look like? Who will I eat with in the chow hall? What about gangs in federal prisons? Will I need money in prison? If so, how much? Will I be forced to work? If so, what kind of job will I get? Can I use the bathroom at any time day or night? Will I be able to access the Internet or send email? What about listening to music?

Glenn Alan Cheney

Prison Literature

Some of the world's greatest writers have done time. In fact, some have done time for being great writers. Inevitably, some of the world's greatest literature—philosophy, fiction, memoir, commentary—has been either composed in or inspired by prison.

- Marco Polo wrote about his travels to China while imprisoned in Genoa.
- Miguel de Cervantes, captured by Barbary pirates, spent five years as a galley slave.
- Sir Walter Raleigh wrote his *History of the World, Volume 1* while held in the Tower of London.
- John Bunyan, arrested for unapproved preaching, wrote *The Pilgrim's Progress* in prison.
- Martin Luther translated the *New Testament* into German and wrote many polemical works while he hid from authorities at Wartburg Castle.
- Marquis de Sade wrote several novellas, volumes of essays, and plays during an 11-year term in the Bastille.
- Napoleon Bonaparte wrote his memoir while held at St. Helena island.
- Fyodor Dostoevsky was inspired to write *The House of the Dead* while serving four years of hard labor in Siberia.

- Oscar Wilde wrote his essay "De Profundis" while in jail for "unnatural acts" with other men.

- e.e. cummings wrote *The Enormous Room* in a French prison during World War I.

- Adolf Hitler wrote *Mein Kampf* while in prison.

- O. Henry wrote 14 stories while doing time for embezzlement.

- Iranian Mahmoud Dowlatabadi wrote *Missing Soluch* in his head while in prison for writing things that revolutionaries read.

- Albert Speer wrote *Inside the Third Reich* and *Spandau: The Secret Diaries* while at Spandau prison.

- Nawal El Saadawi, "The Simone de Beauvoir of the Arab world" wrote *Memoirs from the Women's Prison* while under arrest for publishing a feminist magazine.

- Martin Luther King wrote "Letter from the Birmingham Jail" during one of his 29 arrests.

- Wally Lamb helped several female prisoners write auto-biographical essays in *Couldn't Keep It to Myself* and *I'll Fly Away*.

Other imprisoned writers include Chris Abani, Nelson Algren, Precious Bedell, Boethius, Ernest Booth, Kathy Boudin, Vera Figner Antonio Gramsci, Jean Genet, Hugo Grotius, George Lester Jackson, Robert Lowell, Donald Lowrie, Lady Constance Lytton, Caesarina Kona Makhoere, Danny Martin, Patricia McConnel, Raimundo Montecuccoli, Kate Richards O'Hare, Madame Roland, Béatrice Saubin, Ken Saro-Wisa, Agnes Smedley, Ngugi wa Thiongo, Pramoedya Ananta Toer, Jim Tully, and Krystyna Wituska.

Glenn Alan Cheney

In Nigeria

In January of 2017, Nigeria had 47,229 people in prison while waiting for trial. That's from a total prison population of 67,586. According to the vice president of Nigeria, Prof. Yemi Osinbajo, their average wait was about three years.[1]

Three years is a long time in a Nigerian prison. According to the U.S. "Country Reports on Human Rights Practices for 2015," "Prison and detention center conditions remain harsh and life-threatening. Prisoners and detainees, the majority of whom had not been tried, were reportedly subjected to extra-judicial execution, torture, gross overcrowding, food and water shortages, inadequate medical treatment, deliberate and incidental exposure to heat and sun, and infrastructure deficiencies that led to wholly inadequate sanitary conditions that could result in death. Guards and prison officials reportedly extorted inmates or levied fees on them to pay for food, prison maintenance, and release from prison. Female inmates in some cases faced the threat of rape."[2]

---

1   PM News, February 7, 2018 https://www.pmnewsnigeria. com/2017/01/30/47229-detainees-awaiting-trial-in-nigerian-prisons-osibanjo/

2   "Deplorable Conditions in Nigerian Prisons," Daily Trust (editorial), May 13, 2016 dailytrust.com.ng

No Saint for San Quentin

San Quentin is not named after St. Quentin, a Roman mission-ary who was arrested for his preaching, manacled, and tortured and then was to be transported and put on trial, except he escaped, then captured, tortured, beheaded, and thrown in a swamp, where his body was later found thanks to his "odor of sanctity." The Quentin of California fame was a Miwok Indian who was captured on what was later known as Point Quentin, where a prison was built in 1852.

Glenn Alan Cheney

Groups and Programs at San Quentin

There's no reason to be bored while doing time at San Quentin. Here are some of the organizations and programs that prisons can use to improve themselves and prepare for a return to outside society.

- AA -- Alcoholics Anonymous
- Alliance for CHANGE -- self-development
- ARC -- addiction recovery counseling
- CenterForce -- peer health counseling
- Change is Possible -- self-development
- CRI -- California Reentry Institute
- Developing a Positive Attitude -- self-development
- Green Life -- environmentally healthy living
- GRIP -- Guiding Rage Into Power
- IMPACT -- enabling positive choices
- Kairos -- spiritual retreat program
- Kid CAT -- lifers convicted as juveniles
- MOMAS -- fostering business and financial literacy
- NA -- Narcotics Anonymous

- No More Tears -- violence prevention
- Non-Violent Communications -- (self-explanatory)
- Over-Comers -- Christian Narcotics Anonymous
- Project REACH -- peer tutoring
- RE Choices -- youth mentoring
- Richmond Project -- issues in the city of Richmond
- San Quentin News (newspaper)
- S.Q. TRUST -- responsibility for self, family, and community
- SQUIRES -- youth mentoring
- The Last Mile -- business and technical literacy
- The Work -- self-development
- Vietnam Veterans -- addressing veterans' issues
- Violence Prevention
- VOEG -- victim-offender restorative justice
- Yoga

Glenn Alan Cheney

Keeping Women Busy

The programs and treatments at York Correctional Institution in Niantic, Conn., include 12-Step recovery programs, day job assignments, trauma recovery, alternatives to violence, anger management, artists in residence, book club, books for babies, Bible studies, Protestant and Catholic choir, Catholic retreats (Kairos, Emmaus, Legion of Mary, Life in the Spirit), literacy, English as a second language, public service projects, Habitat for Humanity, Warm the Baby/Warm the Elderly crocheting, Daybreak Protestant programs, puppy training, exercise classes, Good Works re-entry mentoring, greenhouse work (planting, garden design, etc.), grief and loss recovery, trauma healing for abused women, GED, how to be happy, certified nurse's aide, Islamic studies, Performance Project, childbirth support, library, life skills, Microsoft software, Miracle of Melody, Motivation and Self-Mastery, Overeaters Anonymous, parenting, pre-natal and post-partum education, Project Rap, Quinnipiac University, Weslyan University, and Trinity College for-credit courses, self-esteem, Seven Challenges, sex offender treatment, Sisters Standing Strong, Storybook Project, stress management, textile shop, certified cosmetology and barbering training, [3]culinary arts, adult basic education, business education, computer education, hospitality operations technology, smoking cessation, women's wellness, creative writing, and yoga, and many others.

---

3   http://portal.ct.gov/DOC/Facility/York-CI

Glenn Alan Cheney

The News from San Quentin

From the January 2018 edition of San Quentin News:[4]

YOUTH OFFENDER MIX TAPE CAPTURES
GENERATIONAL TRAUMA OF INCARCERATION

Daniel Gutierrez, 21, says with regret that prison has been the norm in his family. "Everyone has been to jail except my mom."

When I got to San Quentin, I ended up three cells down from where my grandfather was once housed. In the county jail I was in the same dorm my father was once in. I was even on the same (prison) yard with my uncle," said Gutierrez.

A musician, Gutierrez said he shares a parallel life with his grandfather, Jose Moreno, who has been out of prison two decades. He even reflected on that relationship in a rap song, "The Same Prison as My Grandfather," on a San Quentin Youth Offender mix-tape project. Gutierrez uses the song for therapeutic relief and guidance for his future....

---

4   sanquentinnews.com

Drugs and Drones, Eagles and Death Rays

The extent of the use of drugs and alcohol in prisons around the world is largely unknown, but it is estimated that a third of the world's prisoners have managed to ingest drugs during their time behind bars. Many inject drugs for the first time while locked up.[5]

England has seen a sharp rise in the use of drones to drop drugs and other contraband into prison yards. The government called it "a significant new and evolving threat."[6] The Chief Prison Inspectorate for England and Wales reported that drones were a reason for high levels of drug use in certain prisons.

In July 2016, a man received the first prison sentence for using a drone to fly contraband into prisons.[7]

But England has a plan. Actually, it's a Dutch idea, and it seems to be working. Police in Netherlands have been using trained eagles to hunt and intercept illegal drones.[8] The French have been

5   International Drug Policy Consortium, "Drug Policy Guide," 3rd edition, 2016. fileserver.idpc.net/library/IDPC-drug-policy-guide_3-edition_FINAL.pdf

6   "Prison Safety and Reform," a presentation to Parliament, Lord Chancellor and Secretary of State for Justice, Nov. 2016

7   "Man jailed for using drone to fly drugs into prisons," The Guardian, July 21, 2016

8   Trevor Mogg, "The UK may start using eagles to take down drones," *Digital Trends*, Nov. 2, 2016

doing the same. In early 2017, the French military also began to use trained eagles to bring down drones.[9]

But the Brits aren't putting all their eagle eggs in one basket. If eagles can't do the trick, there may be other ways to skin the cat. The alternatives include a bazooka that fires a net,[10] a net-carrying interceptor drone being used by police in Japan,[11] and an anti-drone death ray.[12]

9   Trevor Mogg, "France is now using golden eagles to take down rogue drones,"*Digital Trends*, Feb. 15, 2017

10   Gian Volpicelli, "SkyWall 100: An Anti-drone Bazooka, Ars Technica, March 10, 2016. arstechnica.com

11   Rhiannon Williams, "Tokyo police are using drones with nets to catch other drones," The Telegraph, Dec. 11, 2015.

12   "Anti-drone 'death ray' can blast vehicles out of the sky from a mile away," The Guardian, Oct. 7, 2015.

Half a Million

Feel like having your soul crushed for an hour and a half? Watch the documentary film "Kids Behind Bars—Real Stories." It tells the stories of a few of the half a million children who are in prisons around the world, from England to Mongolia. It's on YouTube.com.[13]

Other documentaries on YouTube include

- "Lockdown Prison: Kids Behind Bars"
- "The Hardest Kids Prison"
- "Prison: Kids Behind Bars, why are children in prison?"
- "Life in Prisons: Kids Serve LIFE in Prison"
- "Teenagers Serving Life in Prison"
- "America's Youngest Sex Offenders"
- "Kid Criminals"
- "Babies Behind Bars"

---

13   https://www.youtube.com/watch?v=0XOjEqPFwoU

Glenn Alan Cheney

Don't Get Busted in Brazil

Brazil has one of the ugliest prison situations in the world. There may be places with worse prisons, but Brazil ranks fourth in number of prisons with close to 650,000 people behind bars, 42 percent of them just waiting for trial.[14] The conditions are horrific. Prisoners are 30 times more likely to contract tuberculosis. Cells hold many times more than they were built for. A Minister of Justice called the nation's prisons "medieval dungeons."[15] Brazil has the fourth largest prisonpopulation in the world.

The Curado prison complex in Recife, state of Pernambuco, holds some 7,000 prisoners in a facility built for 1,800. A reporter found 60 prisoners in a cell built for six. Cells are left unlocked because prisoners would suffocate if packed in at the same time. Guards cannot enter cell blocks, so keys are entrusted to powerful

14   César Muñoz Acebes, "Brazil's Correctional Houses of Horror," Public Affairs, Jan. 18, 2017.

15   Luísa Martins, "'Presídios do País são masmorras medievais', diz ministro da Justiça," Estado de São Paulo, Nov. 5, 2015.

29

inmates. Conditions are so filthy that leprosy is a problem.[16]

In 2016, during riots at two juvenile facilities in Pernambuco, 11 teens lost their lives and 11 others were injured. One of the dead had been attacked while in handcuffs in solitary confinement. A few days later, an uprising at the Caruau facility in São Paulo left seven teens dead, one of them decapitated.[17]

Gangs control the prisons more than guards do, and their conflicts result in mass killings, beheadings, mutilated bodies, and sometimes mass escapes. An uprising and gang-versus-gang battle in a prison in Manaus resulted in 56 deaths and more than 130 escapes.[18] President Michel Temer called it a "dreadful accident."[19]

---

16   Resolução da Corte Interamericana de Direitos Humanos de 23 de Novembro de 2016

17   Press Release, "IACHR Condemns Acts of Violence in Detention Facilities in Pernambuco, Brazil," Inter-American Commission on Human Rights, Nov. 23, 2016.

18   Camila Henriques et al, "Rebelião em presídio chega ao fim com 56 mortos, diz governo do AM," G1.globo.com, Jan. 6, 2017.

19   Luciana Amaral e Barnardo Caram, "Temer afirma que chacina no presídi de Manaus foi 'acidente pavoroso,'"

Glenn Alan Cheney

All Is Not Bad in Brazil

Brazil is finding success in a very innovative program called the Association for the Protection and Assistance to Convicts (APAC). At APAC prisons, prisoners are given respect and responsibility...and keys to their cells and even the main gate of the prison. Inmates wear their own clothes, prepare their own food, and, believe it or not, provide their own security. There are no guards or weapons. The inmates govern themselves.

And there's no violence. Inmates don't even want to escape. They are in the last years of their sentences, and their ultimate freedom depends on good behavior. Good behavior includes a strict routine of work and study. Some prisoners can leave the prison to do volunteer work for the community, reconstructing the social pact they broke by committing a crime.

The inmates are not called prisoners but *recuperados*, that is, people in recovery. Conditions are much better than in other prisons. The population is limited to avoid crowding. Consequently, recidivism is lower, and so is the cost of operating the prison.

Similar programs are operating in Costa Rica, Chile, and Ecuador.

APAC prisons work. They cost less and actually produce better citizens rather than better criminals. Why aren't there more? For one thing, the program depends on support by the Italian AVSI Foundation. For another, Brazilian politicians tend to put self-interest over concerns for country and people. For another, political will is always hard to sustain when the general population is boiling with anger over criminal violence. For another, communities resist the idea of hosting a prison where, under certain conditions, inmates are allowed to walk out the front gate.[20]

Why aren't there APAC prisons in the United States? Same reasons.

---

20   Jo Griffin, "'I have no thought of escaping': Inside the Brazilian prisons with no guards," The Guardian, April 2, 2018.

Glenn Alan Cheney

Wild Horses Scared Inside

There does seem to be something about the outside of a horse that is good for the inside of a man.

Winston Churchill

Several states are having success with prisons involved with farming, especially the care of animals. Arizona, Colorado, Florida, Kansas, Louisiana, Nevada, Texas, Virginia, and Wyoming have programs involving horses.[21] Some of the programs involve the domestication and training of wild horses, a process known as "gentling." Generally the gentled horses are sold off for adoption. The inmates who are with them are well aware of the similarity of the men's and horses' situation: once wild, now fenced in, eventually to get out. One inmate said, "I look at them like us: I helped the horse become a better person so he can make parole."[22]

An article about the program at the maximum-security prison in

21   Gavin Ehringer and Julie Stein, "Prison Programs Provide Second Chances for Inmates and Horses," The Chronicle of the Horse, Nov. 12, 2012.

22   Steven Kurutz, "Wild Horses and the Inmates Who 'Gentle' Them," New York Times, Oct. 5, 2017.

Florence, CO, said this:

> The horses were just trying to survive. They acted mean and aggressive, but in reality they were scared to death, just like the men. For the first time in the lives of these men, they were shown the undeniable truth about who they were.
>
> They had learned and believed that being tough and vicious was their only hope of survival. But now — just like these beautiful, wild, violent, and unpredictable animals — the men could see that their motive had also been fear. And maybe, just like the horses, they too could change.
>
> Behind their violence, the mustangs were deeply afraid. The inmates identified with that. They saw themselves. They began to feel compassion, an emotion they had probably never known or felt before. They felt it for the horses, they felt it for each other, and they felt it for themselves.
>
> The inmates were trying to gentle the horses, but in truth the horses were gentling the inmates.[23]

---

23   Tim Hayes, "How Wild Horses Made Prison Inmates Realize Something Transformative about Themselves," Huffpost, Dec. 6, 2017.

Glenn Alan Cheney

Tablets for Prisoners

In early 2018 the New York State's Department of Corrections announced that each of the state's 50,300 inmates would be receiving a free tablet computer.

The tablets were to be provided free of charge by a company called JPay, which manufactures the tablets and installs them with free educational materials and books. However, the prisoners would have to pay for any additional downloads, such as apps, games, books, and music. There would also be a charge of 35 cents to send or receive email.

All revenues would go to JPay. There would be no expense to taxpayers.[24] The DoC said that the purposes of the program were to promote education and safety and help families communicate.[25] Prisons are said to be calmer when prisoners are zoned out with tablets, and more communication with families reduces recidivism.

---

24   Jon Campbell, "New York inmates to get free tablet computers," Democrat & Chronicle, Feb. 1, 2018.

25   Erica Bryant, "Guess who's really paying for New York Inmates to use tablets? Their families," Democrat & Chronicle, Feb. 7, 2018.

Maybe Education Works

Bard College's Bard Prison Initiative has been offering college level courses to inmate students in New York State prisons since 2001. The program has been an unquestionable success. Hundreds of inmate students have earned degrees. Only four percent of those who take courses, and 2.5 percent of those who graduate, commit a crime and return to prison after their release. These graduates are not people who normally pursue and earn college degrees. They tend to come from poor communities with limited educational resources. The majority were first arrested when they were children, and few arrived with high school diplomas. But when presented with an opportunity to improve themselves, they take it. In fact, they compete with each other for limited slots in the program. At some of the New York prisons, more than ten percent of the inmates are taking courses.

Now a dozen other colleges are emulating the program at other prisons. The Bard initiative has been reported in the New York Times and the *New York Review of Books*. The *60 Minutes* television program brought the story to millions of people. The program received even more publicity when the Eastern New York Correctional Facility debate team defeated a team from Harvard.[26]

---

26   Katia Hetter, "New York inmates defeat Harvard debate team," CNN, Oct. 7, 2015.

Glenn Alan Cheney

Unfair Education?

Higher education in prisons is proven to work, and the success of the Bard Prison Initiative is no secret. Ex-prisoners become responsible, taxpaying citizens rather than go back to a life of crime. So why aren't all prisons offering college courses and degrees?

Money is certainly one reason. The inmates don't have much of it. Legislators, unable to see that college courses cost less than post-release crime and recidivism, see no reason to educate criminals. Even New York legislators turned down a proposal from Governor Cuomo to dedicate $1 million to finance college education behind bars. Colleges can't easily afford to dedicate professors and materials to a program, so they depend on donations.

But it isn't just the money. The issue has been swept up in a "get tough on crime" controversy, and many feel it isn't fair to educate prisoners when many taxpayers can't afford to go to college.

One of the New York legislators said the governor's proposal was "a slap in the face of honest taxpayers."

A Republican senator from Texas said it was unfair for felons to benefit from Pell grants when low-income students were denied them.

President Clinton signed a crime bill preventing prisoners from using federal funds for college courses, stating, "This bill puts government on the side of those who abide by the law, not those who break it, on the side of the victims, not their attackers."

A college professor whose daughter was murdered, said, "This does not make sense to me. What is the point?"

It's an old argument, that vengeance is sweeter than actually solving a problem.[27]

---

27   "Jonathan Zimmerman, "Scholars Behind Bards," The New York Review of Books, Feb. 23, 2017, and "Alison Leigh Cowan, "Shoots of College Sprout at a Prison," New York Times, Nov. 17, 2009.

Glenn Alan Cheney

Like Little Prisons Where Everyone Can See

Stocks—a hinged device used to restrain a prisoner's ankles and wrists—have been in use since biblical times, but it was in colonial America that stocks had very much the same purpose as prisons: to prevent flight, to punish, and to deter.

The prevention from flight was generally to hold the accused until trial. The punishment was not just physical pain but public humiliation. The two combined to deter others from similar crimes.

In the New Testament, the Book of Acts refers to Paul and Silas, disciples of Jesus who "advocated customs unlawful for Romans," were stripped, beaten with rods, thrown into prison, and then locked into stocks in an inner cell.

Statute of Labourers 1351 required that every town maintain a set of stocks for "unruly artisans."

In colonial times, people locked in stocks could be humiliated, beaten, paddled, whipped, spat upon, smacked with trash, doused with the contents of chamber pots, even tickled by any passerby with such an urge.

A Captain Kemble was sentenced to several hours in the stocks for kissing his wife in public on the sabbath. That he was returning from three years at sea was no excuse.

In Puritan Boston, Edward Palmer was sentenced to an hour in the stocks for the crime of charging too much for the stocks that he had just built.

Being sentenced to stocks is still legal in the United States. In 1989, a town in Arkansas passed a curfew law that would condemn an offender's parents to time in the stocks, though the ordinance was removed because the town did not have or want to pay for stocks. In 2004, the U.S. Court of Appeals upheld public humiliation as a reasonable punishment with the objective of rehabilitation. (No stocks were involved, but a mail thief had to wear a sandwich board stating "I stole mail; this is my punishment."[28]

---

28   James A. Cox, "Colonial Crimes and Punishments," *Colonial Williamsburg Journal*, Spring 2003. Also, United States v. Gementera, (9th circuit, 2004. Also, , Stocks, accessed Jan. 26, 2018, Wikipedia.

Resistance to the PIC

An organization called Critical Resistance is aiming at the complete abolition of prisons. While the organization doesn't claim to have a plan or model for doing so, it has identified a problem—prisons as a result and cause of problems—and is working on a viable solution. Here's a statement from their website, criticalresistance.org:

> The prison industrial complex (PIC) is a term we use to describe the overlapping interests of government and industry that use surveillance, policing, and imprisonment as solutions to economic, social and political problems.
>
> Through its reach and impact, the prison industrial complex helps and maintains the authority of people who get their power through racial, economic and other privileges. There are many ways this power is collected and maintained through the PIC, including creating mass media images that keep alive stereotypes of people of color, poor people, queer people, immigrants, youth, and other oppressed communities as criminal, delinquent, or deviant. This power is also maintained by earning huge profits for private companies that deal with prisons and police forces; helping earn political gains for "tough on crime" politicians; increasing the

influence of prison guard and police unions; and eliminating social and political dissent by oppressed communities that make demands for self-determination and reorganization of power in the US.

PIC abolition is a political vision with the goal of eliminating imprisonment, policing, and surveillance and creating lasting alternatives to punishment and imprisonment.

From where we are now, sometimes we can't really imagine what abolition is going to look like. Abolition isn't just about getting rid of buildings full of cages. It's also about undoing the society we live in because the PIC both feeds on and maintains oppression and inequalities through punishment, violence, and controls millions of people. Because the PIC is not an isolated system, abolition is a broad strategy. An abolitionist vision means that we must build models today that can represent how we want to live in the future. It means developing practical strategies for taking small steps that move us toward making our dreams real and that lead us all to believe that things really could be different. It means living this vision in our daily lives.

Abolition is both a practical organizing tool and a long-term goal.

A free book on the topic is available at http://criticalresistance.org/resources/abolitionist-tools/

Glenn Alan Cheney

History

Île du Diable

Devil's Island was one part of a prison system established by
France in French Guiana and on three islands off its coast.
Previously, prisoners had been kept on hulks and in prison camps.
When Napoleon III took power in 1851, he saw a way to increase the
French population in Guiana, which was failing as a colony. He'd
increase the population with prisoners and use them for labor. Those
who survived their sentence—a small minority—would be required
to remain in the colony. It was called "forced residency."

Most of the prisoners were petty criminals. A few were political
prisoners guilty of criticizing the government. Captain Alfred Drey-
fus, framed as a traitor, was the most famous, sentenced in 1895.
Political prisoners and the worst of violent criminals were assigned
to Devil's Island. Living conditions were not compatible with life.
Prisoners there had a certain freedom to roam since the island was
surrounded by shark-infested waters. Escape was virtually impossible.

A few managed to escape. Anarchist Clément Duval attempted
escape over 20 times in 16 years before succeeding and making his

way to New York City. Four other managed to reach St. Thomas, Virgin Islands. René Belbenoît escaped and wrote two memoirs: Hell on Trial and Fifteen Years among the Living Dead.

Henri Charrière wrote *Papillon*, a bestseller about his escape from Devil's Island. It was later discovered that he'd never been to Devil's Island, that he'd escaped from a mainland prison camp. He based his tale on Clément Duval's escape, but it was mostly fiction.

France didn't stop sending prisoners to the prison complex until 1938, though the prison didn't really close until 1953. Of the estimated 70,000 prisoners who had spent time in the prison complex, only some 2,000 ever saw France again. The last prisoner on Devil's Island when the prison closed refused to leave. He was still there in 1958. Nobody knows his name or what happened to him.[29]

29   David Wallechinsky and Irving Wallace, *The People's Almanac*, Doubleday, 1975.

Easy In, Easy Out

Jack Sheppard (1702-1724) knew how to put the "escape" in "escapade." Before he finished his apprenticeship as a carpenter, he was tempted into a life of crime, not to mention an adventurous relationship with a prostitute much larger than his diminutive self.

At the age of six, little Jack was sold off to a workhouse to learn the trade of making cane-chairs. Over the next 14 years he worked his way up to an apprenticeship in carpentry. But by the age of 20 he'd had enough of the honest life of de facto indentured slavery. He started hanging out at a tavern populated by local thieves. There he fell in love with a prostitute. Her name was Elizabeth Lyon, though everyone knew her as Edgworth Bess. Jack began his criminal career with shoplifting and petty burglary. He had no legal problems until Elizabeth got arrested and thrown into prison. Jack broke in, freed her, and the two of them got away.

A while later, he and his brother committed a burglary. The brother got caught, and since it was his second arrest, he faced possible execution. The only way out was to rat out his brother Jack. When Jack got tempted into a game of skittles at a tavern, somebody fetched the local constable. Jack got arrested and locked in the upper floor of a building. He escaped through the ceiling and lowered himself to the ground with knotted bedclothes.

Within a month he got arrested for picking a pocket. When Bess came to visit him in the local slammer, she got locked up, too. They got transferred to a real prison. Within a day they filed through some window bars and again used bedclothes to lower themselves to the ground. This second escape ensured their working-class heroism.

Two months later a colleague in crime got Bess drunk in a tavern. She revealed where Jack could be found. He was arrested and sentenced to death for his thievery. Five days before his execution date, Bess distracted a guard long enough for Jack to remove an interior window bar and squeeze out. Disguised in women's clothing, he slipped out of the prison and got away.

Too cocky to leave town, he was arrested a few days later. He was put in handcuffs and leg irons in a "strong room," but he soon picked the lock of the handcuffs and, still in leg irons, made his way up a chimney, onto the roof, then through six barred doors to get into the chapel and from there onto the roof of a neighboring house, then down through the house (without awakening anyone) and into the street.

Within two weeks he was captured. This time he was chained to a 300-pound block in a cell under constant observation. He was soon relieved of a pocket knife he was planning to use to cut his gallows rope. An estimated 200,000 people accompanied his trip to the gallows. Due to his light weight, his hanging failed to break his neck, so he was left strangling for 15 minutes. The crowd, fearing he would be dissected—a common fate of the executed— closed in on his body, preventing an attempt by friends to whisk him off to a doctor.[30]

---

30   Jack Sheppard, accessed Oct. 24, 2017, Wikipedia.

Controlling Society Like a Prison

In the late 18th century, English philosopher Jeremy Bentham published an idea for a new kind of prison. It was new in both physical and psychological senses. He called it The Panopticon.

The name derives from a mythological Greek giant named Panoptes. Panoptes was so called because he could see (*-optes*) everything (*pan*). He had 100 eyes and thus was considered the perfect watchman. But one day Panoptes fell asleep and closed all his eyes. Along came the god of messages, Hermes, who bashed his head in.

Bentham's Panopticon prison was designed in a circle with cells around the outside and guards in the center. The guards, or even just one guard, could at any moment observe any prisoner. They could not, however, observe all the prisoners all the time. The prisoners would never know whether they were being observed. Louvered blinders would allow the guards to see the prisoners without the prisoners seeing the guards.

Bentham claimed that the Panopticon would not only save money but reform prisoners. It would save money by minimizing the need for guards. It would reform prisoners by inducing them to behave themselves all the time, not just when they saw a guard nearby. Theoretically, they would take that self-control with them when released.

No such prison has ever been built, though the theory has been applied in prisons and in public venues. People under the eyes of video surveillance cameras never know whether they are being watched. Cameras deployed in certain English cities actually have loudspeakers so distant observers can give information—or orders—to the public. The dystopian rulers in George Orwell's 1984 had cameras installed in all homes and other places. With draconian punishment for misbehavior, citizens would never take a chance that they were not under observation.

The theory of panopticism, therefore, has the potential to shift from control of prisons to control of society, rendering both not much different from each other.[31]

---

31   Panopticon, Jan. 8, 2018, Wikipedia.

Prisons as Social Failures

Q: Are there really architects opposed to the common, quasi-panopticon design of prisons?

A: Yes, for this is America, home of an organization called Architects/Designers/Planners for Social Change (ADPSR —adpsr. org). Here is part of the ADPSR's position on the issue, based on Discipline and Punish: The Birth of the Prison by French philosopher Michel Foucault.[32]

> Foucault believed that disciplinary systems, and prisons in particular (with the Panopticon as the ideal type) were social failures. He considered that the way disciplinary systems crush individuality and individual freedom is antithetical to positive social goals such as rehabilitation and peaceful coexistence. He also saw the inherent cruelty of prison buildings for what they are - spaces where state agents, dedicated to maintaining state power, exact revenge and enforce discipline on those who fail to abide by the system. Given the overwhelming failure of prisons to reduce crime, and the endless catalogue of abuses committed within prisons, ADPSR agrees with Foucault. It is time for architects to find new means of building a just society, and new buildings for a better set of institutions. The disciplinary model of the prison/Panopticon is a failure.

32   http://www.adpsr.org/home/prison_design_and_control retrieved Jan 23, 2018.

The Cat Mule

Some clever—but not quite clever enough—prisoners in a prison in Brazil, attempted to use a cat to smuggle a cell phone, saws, batteries, and drills into the prison.

Guards caught the cat, which was loaded down like a pack mule. The prison's more than 250 inmates were all suspects, though officials were not able to identify any individuals linked to the escape attempt.[33]

---

33   Glenn Alan Cheney, *The Cat Caboodle: A Litter Box of Cat Facts and Curiosities*, citing Alden Mahler Levine, "Jailbreak! Cat caught with saws, drill and phone in Brazil prison," CNN, Jan. 7, 2013.

Patron Saints

Maximilian Kolbe is the patron saint of prisoners. He was a Franciscan friar in Poland when the Germans invaded in 1939. He was arrested briefly, then allowed to return to his monastery. When the Germans caught the monastery publishing anti-Nazi materials, they shut it down and arrested five friars. On May 28, 1941, Kolbe was transferred to the Auschwitz prison camp, where he was designated Prisoner #16670.

In July of that year, three prisoners escaped. To discourage any further escapes, the German picked ten men to be starved to death in an underground bunker. When one of the men pleaded that he had a wife and children, Kolbe volunteered to take his place. Two weeks later, Kolbe was the only man alive. Impatient and in need of the bunker for other purposes, the Germans gave Kolbe a lethal injection of carbolic acid. Kolbe raised his arm to facilitate the execution. He was canonized by the Pope John Paul II, a Pole himself.

Guards have three patron saints in the Catholic ranks.

Peter of Alcantara, a friar in Spain who could pray himself into ecstasy and even levitation. In 1562 he died on his knees while in prayer. He was known for sleeping very little, and when he slept, he slept sitting up. Thanks to his late-night vigilance, he was designated patron saint of night watchmen.

Adrian of Nicomedia is patron saint of soldiers, butchers, and guards. Until 306 A.D. he was a typical Roman pagan working as bodyguard for the emperor. He was present when 22 Christians were put on trial and subsequently imprisoned and subjected to horrific torture. Adrian (a.k.a. Hadrian) asked one of the prisoners how he could withstand such torture. The prisoner quoted Corinthians: "Eye hath not seen, nor ear heard, neither have entered into the heart of man, the things which God hath prepared for them that love him"

Adrian was so impressed that he converted on the spot. He was then imprisoned himself. After repeatedly refusing to renounce his Christianity, he was tortured to death, the last part of which involved smashing his arms and legs on an anvil. His body was supposed to be burned out of existence, but a storm arose, quenched the fire and, for good measure, killed several guards with lightning. Adrian's wife, Natalia, managed to retrieve one of his hands. She took it home and then to Constantinople.[34]

---

34   Orthodoxy Church in America, https://oca.org/saints/all-lives/2013/08/26 Jan. 8, 2018.

Big Leaks at Leavenworth

In 1910, Frank Grigware, a prisoner at Leavenworth held for train robbery, and five other prisoners hijacked a supply locomotive on prison grounds and used it to smash through a gate. The other five were soon recaptured, but Grigware made his way to Canada, where in 1916 he was elected mayor of Spirit River, Alberta.[35]

Basil "The Owl" Banghart escaped from Leavenworth three times. In his long career as a criminal, he was involved in or allegedly involved in car theft, robbery, mail truck armed robbery, a hoax kidnapping, racketeering, tossing a bomb into a bar, brewing wine in a prison, escape not only from Leavenworth but a federal building and a local jail, and—get this—failing to inform the Selective Service of his change of address.[36]

---

35   "A Byte Out of History: The Five-Decade Fugitive Chase," fbi.gov/news/stories/the-five-decade-chase, Jan. 24, 2014.

36   John William Tuohy, "The Owl," AmericanMafia.com, Dec. 2001.

Convict Leases

The 13th Amendment to the U.S. Constitution—the same that does away with slavery, explicitly allows involuntary servitude as punishment for a crime. After the Civil War, states in the south commonly leased out prisoners to private companies, effectively a continuation of slave labor. In 1898, 73 percent of Alabama's state revenues were generated by leased prisoners.[37]

The profitability of such leases motivated states to arrest and convict more blacks. In Nashville, for example, 33 percent of prisoners were African-American when the war ended in 1865. Four years later, it was 64 percent.[38] A contract with the Georgia and Alabama Railroad specified "one hundred able-bodied and healthy Negro convicts" in exchange for $2,500.[39] In Tallahassee, a young man from North Dakota, Martin Tabert, was arrested for vagrancy and leased to the Putnam Lumber Company, where he was flogged to death by the flogging boss, an incident that led to the end of convict leasing in Florida in 1923. Alabama stopped in 1928, and North Carolina ended a similar practice in 1933.[40]

37   Perkinson, Robert. *Texas Tough: The Rise of America's Prison Empire,* 2010.

38   Convict Lease, accessed Feb. 14, 2018, Wikipedia

39   Fairfax Harrison, *A History of the Legal Development of the Railroad System of Southern Railway Company,* 2012.

40   Milfred Fierce, *Slavery Revisited: Blacks and the Southern Convict Lease System, 1865-1933. New York: Africana Studies Research Center, Brooklyn College,* 1994.

LURKING DOUBT

Glenn Alan Cheney

Why

More Prisoners = Less Crime?

✦

C an the drop in crime over the last 10 years be linked to the high rate of incarceration during the same period?

The answer almost seems obvious until the question gets complicated. Various factors can affect crime rates and incarceration rates, so it's hard to determine how effectively incarceration deters crime. An economic recession can cause an increase in crime, making it hard to compare one year with another. Economic recoveries in Baltimore and Houston and other places aren't necessarily happen at the same time or to the same extent, so it's hard to compare crime rates in different places. At the same time, state changes in mandatory sentencing affect incarceration. Likewise, the legalization of marijuana or a change in legal attitudes toward addiction and treatment affects incarceration rates.

A study published by The Sentencing Project found that in three key states—California, New York, and New Jersey—crime dropped substantially even as prison populations declined.

• New York and New Jersey led the nation by reducing prison populations by 2 percent between 1999 and 2012. The national average saw an increase of 10 percent.

• California downsized its prison population by 23 percent between 2006 and 2012. During that period, the national average saw a decline of just one percent.

• During these periods of "decarceration," violent crime decreased in those states far more than in the rest of the country. Between 1999 and 2012, New York's and New Jersey's violent crime rate fell by 31 percent and 30 percent respectively. The national average was a decrease of 26 percent. Between 2006 and 2012, California's violent crime rate dropped by 21 percent, slightly more than the national decline of 19 percent.

• Numbers were similar for property crime, though California's rate declined by 13 percent, a little less than the national average of 15 percent.

The study found "no reason why a reduction of 25 percent should be considered the maximum that might be achieved." It pointed out that even if every state managed such reductions in prison population, the United States would still have an incarceration rate three to six times higher than those of most industrialized nations.[41]

---

41   Marc Mauer and Nazgol Ghandnoosh, "Fewer Prisoners, Less Crime: A Tale of Three States, The Sentencing Project, July 23, 2014 www.sentencingproject.org/publications/fewer-prisoners-less-crime-a-tale-of-three-states/

Population Explosion

According to the Institute for Criminal Policy Research, prison populations have been increasing rapidly all over the world, but not everywhere.[42]

- Total prison population in 2017 was about 10 million.

- From 2000 to 2015, the prison population of Oceania increased by 59 percent.

- In that period, the U.S. prison population increased by 41 percent.

- In that period, the Asian prison population increased by 29 percent.

- In that period, African prison population increased by 15 percent.

- In that period, the European prison population decreased by 21 percent.

- Much of the decline in Europe was due to a drastic reduction

---

42   Jessica Jacobson, Catherine Heard, Helen Fair, "Prison: Evidence of its use and over-use from around the world," Institute for Criminal Policy Research, University of London, 2017. prisonstudies.org/world-prison-brief

in Russia, where numbers fell from about one million in 2000 to 640,000 in 2015.

• Brazil's prison population increased 20-fold from about 30,000 in 1973 to 600,000 in 2017.

• The number of prisoners in England and Wales increased from 40,000 in 1975 (a rate of 81 per 100,000 people) to 87,000 in 2012 (a rate of 153 per 100,000.)

• The U.S. prison population peaked in 2008 at over 2.3 million, accounting for a full fifth of the world's prisoners.

• The prisoner rates (prisoners per 100,000 people) were highest in the U.S. (666 per) and Thailand (428).

• Prisoner rates were lowest in Netherlands (61) and India (33).

The ICPR report listed several reasons the over-use of incarceration is counter-productive. It found that over-use:

• leads to crowded, inhumane, degrading conditions,

• worsened rehabilitation outcomes,

• disproportionately harmed the poor and marginalized, whose families can least afford the absence of a wage-earner or parent,

• reduces the prison system's capacity to deal with the few who really need to be isolated from society,

• increases the risks to prisoners, prison staff, and the general population,

• imposes enormous costs on public funds, and

• impedes economic development.

Some Findings

• Prison education reduces recidivism more than boot camps, "shock" incarceration, or vocational training.[43]

• Prison education reduces recidivism by 29 percent.[44]

• Only six percent of corrections spending goes to prison programs (of which education is just one).[45]

• Fifteen prison systems account for 89 percent of the nation's prisoners taking postsecondary classes and awarded 96 percent of college degrees.[46]

• Lack of funding is the most common barrier to enrolling prisoners in college courses.[47]

• A $1 million investment in incarceration will prevent about 350 crimes. The same investment in prison education will prevent more than 600 crimes.[48]

---

43   Lawrence W. Sherman et. al, "Preventing Crime: What Works, What Doesn't, What's Promising," National Institute of Justice, 1998.

44   Stephen Steurer, Linda Smith, and Alice Tracy, "Three State Recidivism Study," Correctional Education Association, 2001

45   Wendy Erisman and Jeanne Bayer Contardo, "Learning to Reduce Recidivism: A 50-State Analysis of Post-secondary Correctional Education Policy," Institute for Higher Education Policy, 2005.

46   ibid

47   ibid

48   A. Bazos and J. Hausman, "Correctional Education as a Crime Control

- Post-secondary prison education increases societal productivity, increases tax revenues, and decreases reliance on government support.[49]

- Changes in behavior can be attributed to improved cognitive capacity and to the prisoner feeling human again by engaging in an activity as commonplace as going to classes.[50]

- Post-secondary education in prisons can break down racial barriers that are a major cause of disciplinary problems.[51]

- Children of the women enrolled in the Bedford Hills College Program expressed pride in their mothers' academic achievements, were inspired to take their own education more seriously and were more motivated to attend college themselves.[52]

Program," UCLA School of Public Policy and Social Research, 2004.

48   Institute for Higher Education Policy, "The Investment Payoff," *Institute for Higher Education Policy*, 2005.

50   "Education from the Inside Out: The Multiple Benefits of College Programs in Prison," Correctional Association of New York, 2009.

51   Wendy Erisman and Jeanne Bayer Contardo, "Learning to Reduce Recidivism: A 50-state analysis of post-secondary correctional education policy," *The Institute for Higher Education Policy*, Nov. 2005.

52   ibid

High Rent Districts

How much does it cost to incarcerate in various prisons?

The average cost of incarceration for Federal inmates in Fiscal Year 2015 was $31,977.65 ($87.61 per day). The average annual cost to confine an inmate in a Residential Re-entry Center for Fiscal Year 2015 was $26,082.90 ($71.46 per day).[53]

The average cost of incarceration in a state prison averages about $33,849 per year. The most expensive prisons, per capita incarcerata, were New York ($69,355), California ($64,642), Connecticut ($62,159), New Jersey ($61,603), and Rhode Island (($58,564).[54]

The average annual cost of holding an inmate in a New York City jail in 2017 was about $143,130 per year. In 2017, total cost of the city's jails hit a record at $1.36 billion.[55]

---

53   Federal Register, from Notice of Prisons Bureau on July 19, 2016.https://www.federalregister.gov/documents/2016/07/19/2016-17040/annual-determination-of-average-cost-of-incarceration

54   Ngoc Nuynh, "Report: Cost per prisoner in New York tops other states," newyorkupstate.com, July 26, 2017.

55   Yoav Gonen, "City jail costs hit new record despite drop in inmates," New York Post, Nov. 14, 2017.

Glenn Alan Cheney

The Real Cost

A commonly cited figure for the cost of incarceration is $80 billion, but that is only the cost of operating corrections facilities. A study conducted at Washington University measured 23 different associated costs and came up with an aggregate burden of about $1 trillion—11 times more than the commonly reported cost. More than half of the aggregate cost is borne by families, children, and community members who had committed no crime. Among the costs outside of government "corrections" budgets are:

• Foregone wages of prisoners ($33,066 each, average, in 2014 dollars)

• Reduced lifetime earnings due to incarceration record (10-40 percent)

• Cost of injuries suffered in prison

• Higher mortality rate for released prisoners (3.5 times higher than average)

• Increased infant mortality (40% higher for children of prisoners)

• Increased criminality of children of prisoners ($130.6 billion)

• Visitation, eviction, and moving costs

• Family debt caused by incarceration

- Adverse health effects on families (depression, PTSD, suicide)
- Effect on children's education level and subsequent lifetime wages ($30 billion)
- Children rendered homeless by parental imprisonment ($14,400 each, excluding cost of psychological harm)
- Homelessness of released prisoners (25-50% of homeless people)
- Decreased property values around prisons
- Criminogenic nature of prisons (crime born of prison experience, $285.8 billion)
- Divorce (rates are tripled, totaling $17.7 billion)

The study also found the $80 billion figure to be low because it didn't represent pension obligations, health care benefits for staff, and health care provided to inmates. The more accurate figure is $91.1 billion.

The study did not figure in the benefits of incarceration, such as crime avoided by deterrence and incapacitation.[56]

---

56   Michael McLaughlin et al, "The Economic Burden of Incarceration in the U.S., Institute for Advancing Justice Research and Innovation, Washington University, St. Louis, October 2016.

Glenn Alan Cheney

Clink, Inc.

Governments often contract a private-sector company to run its corrections programs. In some cases, a company owns the prison. In others, it administers a prison owned by a government. In either case, these corporations have a vested interested in a high prison population.

In 2016, the nation's largest imprisonment company, the Corrections Corporation of America (CCA), changed its name to Core-Civic. The change was an apparent attempt to shed the bad image it acquired when an inspector general found substandard living conditions, inadequate medical care, and higher rates of violence at 14 prisons run by the CCA and other companies. The company explained that it was transforming itself from corrections and detention to "a wider range of government solutions."

At the time of the name-change, the CCA was housing some 70,000 prisoners in more than 70 prisons or jails.[57] It owned 50 of the facilities. In 2015, the company reaped a profit of more than

---

57   Casey Tolan, "The largest private prison company in America is changing its name—but can't escape a troubled record," Splinter News, Oct. 28, 2016.

$3,300 per prisoner. Part of its profit is made possible by "occu-pancy guarantees" that require the government to provide a certain number of prisoners. At one facility, the government is obliged to maintain an occupancy of 96 percent. Long sentences, mandatory sentences, stringent laws, and recidivism are means of guaranteeing a supply of prisoners.

The biggest investors in CCA in 2016 were the Vanguard Group, Blackrock, FMR, New South Capital management, Pruden-tial Financial, and Bank of New York Mellon Corp.[58] Meanwhile, Pershing Square Capital Management, Systematic Financial Man-agement, General Electric, Columbia University, and many other in-vestors divested themselves of all CCA stock and in many cases all private prison company stock.[59]

58   https://www.nasdaq.com/symbol/cxw/institutional-holdings. Retrieved Feb. 19, 2018.

59   "The Corrections Corporation of America, by the Numbers," *Mother Jones*, July/August 2016.

Glenn Alan Cheney

Four Justifications for Imprisonment,
None Good

Rehabilitation

Theory: The experience of incarceration will teach criminals a lesson. Upon release, they will be law-abiding citizens.

Reality: Incarceration alone does not improve the character or attitude of criminals.

Deterrence

Theory: Severe punishment, such as long prison sentences, will scare potential criminals away from criminal acts.

Reality: Studies show that high incarceration rates increase crime or have no measurable effect. Crime apparently increases because prisons tend to a) educate prisoners in the art of criminality, b) create anti-social attitudes, c) break up communities, d) break up families, e) prevent released prisoners from finding work.[60]

Incapacitation

Theory: Criminals cannot commit crimes while they are prison.

Reality: Prisons are incubators of crime. Criminals continue

---

60   Steven Raphael and Michael A. Stoll, *Do Prisons Make Us Safer?: The Benefits and Costs of the Prison Boom*. Russell Sage Foundation, 2009.

criminal activity while in prison. Upon release, they are more likely
to commit crimes.

<u>Retribution</u>

Theory: Prison is a form of vengeance. Victims and society are
pleased to see perpetrators suffer what they deserve.

Reality: Vengeance—"pay-back"—does not create some kind
of balance, nor does it negate the effects of the crime, nor does it
deter criminals from criminal acts in the future. To the contrary, it
leaves them angered and...seeking revenge! Future crimes are more
likely and more severe. Ultimately, vengeance through incarceration
causes communities to suffer.[61]

---

61   Prisons, accessed Jan. 12, 2018, Wikipedia.

Glenn Alan Cheney

Highest and Lowest Rates of Incarceration

According to the most recent data available for each country, these are the nations with the highest and lowest rates of prison populations, that is, prisoners per 100,000 population, according to World Prison Brief.[62]

Rank	Nation	Rate per 100,000
1.	Seychelles	738
2.	USA	666
3.	El Salvador	598
4.	Turkmenistan	583
7.	Cuba	510
15.	Russia	419
26.	Brazil	322
37.	Iran	287
133.	China	118
203.	Japan	45
222. (lowest)	Guinea Bissau	10

---

62   prisonstudies.org, retrieved Jan 18, 2018

Federal Prison Industries

Federal Prison Industries, also known as UNICOR, is a corporation owned by the U.S. government. It was established in 1934 to give federal prisoners an opportunity to learn a trade and make a little money. By federal law, all able-bodied federal prisoners who are not a security risk are required to work for either their prison or at a UNICOR factory. In 2016, some 17,900 prisoners worked at 66 UNICOR factory operations in 52 prisons, earning between 23 cents and $1.15 per hour. UNICOR produces more than 100 products, most of which are sold to federal agencies. Prisoners with court-ordered restitution obligations must use at least half of their earnings for those debts. U.S. manufacturers can use UNICOR to manufacture products if the company is repatriating operations from overseas, in which case costs are set at those of offshore sites.[63]

---

63   Federal Prison Industries, accessed Feb. 14, 2018, Wikipedia.

Glenn Alan Cheney

Some Stats to Think About

S ome national statistics for the United States.[64]

• One percent of released killers kill a second time, and 99 percent don't.

• Over 70 percent of released robbers and burglars commit the same crime again.[65]

• 85 percent of prisoners are involved in drugs, but only 11 percent receive treatment.

• Among 16-24 year olds, high school dropouts are six times more likely to be imprisoned.

• Dropouts in that group are 63 times more likely to be imprisoned than people who earned a Bachelor's degree.

• Participation in a prison education program reduces recidivism by 63 percent.

---

64   *Reentry: From Prison to the Streets, Making it Work*, New Jersey Reentry Corporation, September 2017.

65   Dana Goldstein, "The Misleading Math of 'Recidivism': Even the Supreme Court gets it wrong," *The Marshall Project*, Dec. 4, 2014.

Mass Incarceration Explained?

A report from The Sentencing Project, written by three university professors, found that in 2016, an estimated 6.1 million Americans were not eligible to vote due to a felony conviction. That's up from 1.17 million in 1976, 3.34 million in 1996, and 5.85 million in 2010.[66]

Other key findings:

• Approximately 2.5 percent of the total U.S. voting age population—one in every 40 adults—is disenfranchised due to a felony conviction.

• Individuals who have completed their sentences in the twelve states that disenfranchise people post-sentence make up over 50 percent of the entire disenfranchised population, totaling almost 3.1 million people.

• In six states (AL, FL, KY, MS, TN and VA), the rate is more than seven percent of adults.

• Florida—that crucial state that determines presidential elec-

---

66   Christopher Uggen, et al, "6 Million Lost Voters: State-level Estimates of Felony Disenfranchisement, 2016," The Sentencing Project, 2016. https://felonvoting.procon.org/sourcefiles/sentencing-project-felony-disenfranchisement-2016.pdf

tions—accounts for 1.5 million, about 27 percent of the disenfranchised in America.

• One in 13 African-Americans is disenfranchised, four times the number of non-African-Americans.

• In 1980, only nine states disenfranchised more than five percent of their African-American population. In 2016, 23 states did so.

• In FL, KY, TN, and VA, more than 20 percent of African-Americans are disenfranchised.

• Maine and Vermont are the only states that have no restrictions on felons voting. Even prisoners can vote.

• The total number of disenfranchised citizens tripled since roughly the beginning of the civil rights movement. In 1960, it was 1,762,582. In 2016 it hit 6,106,327.

• A "significant majority" of Americans favor voting rights for people on probation or parole or otherwise completing their sentence. If those rights were restored to all released prisoners, 77 percent of the disenfranchised would be able to vote. That's 4,701,871 people.

Trouble in New Jersey

New Jersey has prison problems, and serious reform may be the only solution.[67]

• In 2017, New Jersey had some 41,000 people in federal, state, or local prisons and jails.

• The ratio of black to white prisoners was 12.2:1, more than twice the national average of 5:1.

• The state spends over $1 billion on "corrections" each year.

• In 2017, incarceration cost an average of $53,681 per prisoner per year. (Tuition at Princeton is $43,450. At Rutgers, it's $14, 238.)

• Parole costs an average of $6,349, about a tenth the cost of incarceration.

• Over half of released prisoners are arrested again within three years.

• 37.2 percent of released prisoners do not have a high school diploma.

• 92.3 percent have no college education.

---

67   "Reentry: From Prison to the Streets—Making It Work." NJ Reentry corporation, September 2017.

• At least a third and possibly half of individuals with medical conditions are not treated while incarcerated.

• 41 percent "max out," serving their entire sentence, almost twice the 22 percent national average.

• In 2003, New Jersey had the highest proportion of drug offenders in the country.

• Not counting arrest and court costs, In 2017 the state spent $182,051,328 to incarcerate people who had been released from prison in 2011 and re-incarcerated by 2014—enough to educate 9,265 children for a year.

• New Jersey loses about $71,218,455 in taxes each year due to people in prison rather than working.

• Over half of New Jersey prisoners have a chronic medical condition.

Banned Books

The Texas Department of Criminal Justice bans some 10,000 books from its prison system.[68] Among the prohibited titles: *A Charlie Brown Christmas (pop-up edition)*, *The Color Purple*, *Memoirs of a Geisha*, *A Time to Kill*, *To Kill a Mockingbird*, *MapQuest Road Atlas*, *The Daily Show with Jon Steward Presents America: A Citizen's Guide to Democracy Inaction*, *Women Behind Bars: The Crisis of Women in the U.S. Prison System*, *Where's Waldo*, *Game of Thrones*, *Uncle Tom's Cabin*, *Freakonomics*, *Brokeback Mountain*, *Big Sur*, Dante's *Inferno*, *All the Dave Barry You Could Ever Want*, *The Boys of Summer*, the 1908 Sears, Roebuck catalog, and many titles by such authors as Jenna bush, Noam Chomsky, John Gisham, Langston Hughes, Philip Roth, Salman Rushdie, Studs Terkel, and Sojourner Truth.

Among the 248,000 books allowed: *Lolita, Mein Kampf,* and David Duke's *My Awakening*.

In 2018 the Department began a review of banned and permitted titles.

---

68   Matthew Haag, "Texas Prisons Ban 10,000 Books. No 'Charlie Brown Christmas' for Inmates," New York Times, Dec. 7, 2017.

Glenn Alan Cheney

Damage Control

A Better Place to Spend a Dollar

Long prison sentences may feel good to angry victims of crime, but they don't make anyone any safer, at least not for long. A ten-year penalty isn't twice as effective at preventing crime as a five-year penalty. People of criminal tendency are notoriously poor at thinking long-term. They also presume that they aren't going to get caught. Consequences in the immediate future are well within their vision. The certainty of punishment deters them far more than the severity of the punishment. A dollar spent on policing and other crime prevention efforts is 20 percent more effective than a dollar spent on imprisonment.[69]

---

69   "Too Many prisons make bad people worse. There is a better way," *The Economist*, May 27, 2017.

Glenn Alan Cheney

Criminals as Artists

From *Art Therapy: An Introduction to the Use of Art as a Therapeutic Technique,* chapter titled "Art Therapy in Prisons," by Joyce Laing, edited by Tessa Daily.

...Surprisingly, of all the professionals—the doctors, the social workers, the psychologists, or the teachers—who work in a supportive role with the prisoners, it is the artist who may have the closest personality traits. For it seems there may be underlying links in the drive of certain offenders and that of the creative artist.

While labeled as deviants, many offenders are inventive, ingenious, quick-witted and have great vitality. It may be that the creative aspects of the criminal have, for reasons of background experience or psychological make-up, been misdirected towards destructive ends. If the art therapist can channel these talents in a positive, creative direction, the offender will experience a new perception of the self and where he belongs in society. Over the weeks in which the art work is being produced, step by step, an alteration in his previous thinking pattern will take place. The more he becomes engrossed in art, the less likely will he be content to see himself just as a criminal who is destroying his own potential prospects and the lives of his family, as well as being a menace to everyone else. Art opens so many doors in life.

Where Prisoners Are
Treated Like Adults

When you think about it, inmates are treated like children. They are relieved of all responsibility. They have "parents" watching them constantly. They are told what to do. If they don't obey, they are punished. They are not trusted with sharp objects. Their food is prepared for them. And after a certain number of years, they are declared "grown up" and, for better or worse, released to the world.

Too often it's for the worse. They soon fail at adulthood. A high percentage—the numbers vary widely according to jurisdiction—end up back in prison. There they return to a life free of responsibility and decision.

Norway has figured out that forcing extreme childhood on prisoners doesn't work. At Bastoy prison, inmates are expected to make their own decisions, think ahead, take responsibility, control their impulses, and enjoy the benefits of work. If they want food, they have to make it. If they want better food, they have to tend to crops. If they want to lie on the beach, they have to clean the beach. If they want to make furniture, they have to go cut down a tree. They are entrusted with tools that could easily be made into weapons, everything from hammers to chain saws.

And if they want to escape, they can. There are no walls or razor wire. But who would want to escape from what's been called "the world's nicest prison"?

Completing a sentence at Bastoy (inmates have to earn the right to be transferred there) may not give a crime victim the full pleasure of vengeance, but it results in a better person who is far less likely to commit another crime. They leave Bastoy with a marketable skill and a track record of self-control and responsibility. Only 20 percent are back in the can within two years, half the rate of the United States. Result: a safer community.

As Norway sees it, the issue is a mutually exclusive set of choices: What is the purpose of imprisonment—public safety or revenge? Until someone thinks of some other purpose, public safety is the most beneficial for society.[70]

---

70   "Too Many prisons make bad people worse. There is a better way." *The Economist,* May 27, 2017

Solitary

Solitary confinement was originally an idea of Quakers who saw it as a merciful alternative to public whippings. Isolation was less obviously painful, and it gave inmates a chance to meditate on their wrongdoing. But it didn't take long for the Quakers to see the detrimental effects. In 1826, Alex de Tocqueville observed them, too, when a New York prison tried putting all prisoners in solitary. He wrote, "This experiment, of which the favorable results had been anticipated, proved fatal for the majority of prisoners. It devours the victims incessantly and unmercifully; it does not reform, it kills."[71]

Solitary confinement can provoke so many physical and psychiatric problems that it is considered a form of torture.

Due to lack of exercise, it can cause high blood pressure, migraine headaches, profuse sweating, abdominal pain, neck pain, back pain, muscle stiffness, heart palpitations, weight loss, and changes to brain physiology.

But the most serious and painful consequences are in the mind.

---

71   Elizabeth Vasiliades, "Solitary Confinement and International Rights: Why the U.S. Prison System Fails Global Standards," *American University International Law Review*, Vol 21, Issue 1, 2005.

After a period of confinement, prisoners experience hallucinations and pseudohallucinations[72], hypersensitivity to stimuli, aggressive fantasies, overt paranoia, inability to concentrate, lack of impulse control, confusional psychosis, dissociative tendencies, agitation, aimless violence, delusions, irrational anger, social withdrawal, depression, suicidal ideation, feelings of helplessness, self-mutilation, suicide. They start to babble and shriek. They've been known to smear themselves with feces, bang their heads on walls, and scrub at imaginary bugs. A few develop Ganser syndrome, which is characterized by nonsensical talk, echolalia and echopraxia (the imitation someone else's speech behavior, respectively).

Often mentally ill inmates are the ones who end up in solitary confinement. The confinement tends to worsen, not improve, their symptoms.[73]

In one lawsuit (Ruiz v. Johnson) a judge ruled that "Solitary confinement units are virtual incubators of psychoses—seeding illness in otherwise healthy inmates and exacerbating illness in those already suffering from mental infirmities."

Prisoners have been put in solitary not as punishment but for isolation required due to sexual orientation, race, and religion.

Estimates of the number of prisoners in solitary at a given moment range from 20,000 to 80,000. The numbers range widely because of the difficulty of defining "solitary confinement."

The Supreme Court has never taken a position on whether solitary confinement is unconstitutional.

---

72 That is, hallucinations that a subject knows are not real.

73 Kirsten Weir, "Alone, in 'the hole'," *Monitor on Psychology*, American Psychological Association, May 2012.

Numbers in the Box

In the US, over 65,000 prisoners were held in prolonged solitary confinement (defined by the Nelson Mandela Rules as more than 15 consecutive days in solitary), with 3,000 held there for over six years (half of these in Texas). A 2016 report on New York State prisons demonstrated a racial bias in the use of solitary confinement, showing that Black and Latino prisoners are disciplined at up to twice the rate of white prisoners and for longer.

While the use of solitary confinement in the U.S. has been decreasing in recent years, there were at least 67,442 inmates in the U.S. locked in their cells for 22 or more hours a day in the fall of 2015, according to a report released by the Association of State Correctional Administrators (ASCA) and Yale Law School.[74]

The report, "Aiming to Reduce Time-in-Cell," gives a significant, albeit incomplete, snapshot of the use of solitary confinement

---

74   "Aiming to Reduce Time-In-Cell: Reports from Correctional Systems on the Numbers of Prisoners in Restricted Housing and on the Potential of Policy Changes to Bring About Reforms," Association of State Correctional Administrators and The Arthur Liman Public Interest Program, Yale Law School, Nov. 2016.

in the U.S., which is an outlier among countries in its use of the widely condemned practice. The census includes federal and state inmates placed in any form of "restricted housing" for at least 22 hours a day for more than 15 consecutive days. It did not include local and county jails, federal immigration detention centers, and juvenile and military detention centers, meaning the number could be higher.

Information for the report was provided by 41 jurisdictions. They reported on length of stay, gender, race, age, and mental illness for a sample population of over 54,000 inmates who had spent time in solitary. Of those, 29 percent spent one to three months in solitary confinement. At the other extreme, 11 percent endured three continuous years or more in isolation. Among all respondents, the share of prisoners in solitary in a given facility ranged from under one percent to more than 28 percent of the general population.[75]

---

75   Juleyka Lantigua-Williams, "More Prisons are Phasing out the 'Box,'" *The Atlantic*, Dec. 1, 2016

A Blink of Time

Rick Raemisch, the executive director of Colorado Department of Corrections, had himself locked in solitary confinement—or, as they say in Colorado, "ad seg"— for 20 hours. In his words, it was "just a blink" of time compared with the average of 23 months that Colorado prisoners spend in isolation when sent there, and that's a blink to the 20 years that some prisoners spend there. He wrote about the experience in an op-ed in the New York Times.[76]

> First thing you notice is that it's anything but quiet. You're immersed in a drone of garbled noise — other inmates' blaring TVs, distant conversations, shouted arguments. I couldn't make sense of any of it, and was left feeling twitchy and paranoid. I kept waiting for the lights to turn off, to signal the end of the day. But the lights did not shut off. I began to count the small holes carved in the walls. Tiny grooves made by inmates who'd chipped away at the cell as the cell chipped away

76   Rick Raemisch, "My Night in Solitary," New York Times, Feb. 20, 2014.

at them....

The main light in my cell block eventually turned off, and I fell into a fitful sleep, awakening every time a toilet flushed or an officer yanked on the doors to determine they were secure....

"When I finally left my cell at 3 p.m., I felt even more urgency for reform. If we can't eliminate solitary confinement, at least we can strive to greatly reduce its use. Knowing that 97 percent of inmates are ultimately returned to their communities, doing anything less would be both counterproductive and inhumane.

Can Architects Help?

A study of Dutch prisons found that, of five architectural styles, the radial, panopticon format (often in leaky, dungeon-like conditions featuring solitary confinement) was most likely to cause prisoners to feel estranged from guards. Prisoners in more communal, campus-like settings were more likely to have supportive relationships with guards. The good staff-prisoner relationships were seen as important for the manageability and safety in prisons.

On the other hand, a study conducted among males at Texas prisons found that architectural design had no effect on violence in the prison, though nonviolent behavior problems appeared to be lower.

But then, Netherlands and Texas are two very different places, the Dutch and Texans two very different peoples.[77]

---

77   Robert G. Morris and John L. Worrall, "Prison Architecture and Inmate Misconduct: A Multilevel Assessment," *Crime & Delinquency,* Nov. 7, 2010, and Ryan Jacobs, "How Prison Architecture Can Transform Inmates' Lives," Pacific Standard, June 17, 2014.

In Case You Ever Need to Know

An anonymous blogger who identified himself as X-Con offers these 8 rules for surviving prison.[78]

1. Respect other inmates. Don't call anyone names. Don't cut in line. Don't reach over someone's plate. Don't touch another inmate's stuff. Do not steal.

2. Don't join a gang. In most prisons, you can avoid them. If you do join, you cannot opt out later, and you will have to commit crimes.

3. Do not do drugs or get involved in smuggling.

4. Do not gamble.

5. Do not engage in homosexuality. AIDS is rampant, and jealousy can be deadly.

6. Do not talk to guards at all about anything—not the weather, not the things you've seen.

7. Stay busy with positive activities—exercise, classes, reading, jobs.

8. Get God in your life. Reading the Bible will make you feel better, you'll associate with better people, and it looks good to the parole board.

---

78   https://soapboxie.com/government/rules-how-to-survive-prison

The Perfect Gift for Someone
Who Has Nothing

There aren't many things you can send to a prisoner, but those few things can be deeply meaningful. Each facility has its own rules, and they are probably available online.

1. Letters and Messages.

Many prisons allow prisoners to receive email. Note that these messages are usually reviewed by staff.

Physical mail, especially hand-written, is especially appreciated. The mail is probably reviewed by staff. Do not include staples, paper clips, perfume, cash, or, of course, contraband. Just send sheets of paper, nothing more.

2. Money.

You cannot send cash to an inmate, but facilities usually allow deposits into accounts. There are limits on totals. Inmates can only buy items from the commissary. These include toiletries, snacks, stamps, envelopes, etc.

3. Photos.

Photos bring the outside world into the cell. They can include not just portraits of loved ones but pictures of neighborhoods, pets, and events. There may be limits on quantities and sizes. No frames. No porn. No hidden messages. Write inmate's name and other ID information on the back.

4. Reading Material

Since reading material is considered helpful for rehabilitation, prisons generally allow books and magazines to be sent to prisoners. Often they have to come straight from a publisher or bookstore. Certain topics are prohibited. Paperbacks only.

5. Celebratory Cards

Birthday cards and such are generally allowed, but note: no "singing" cards with electronics, no heavy cardboard stock, no pop-ups, no multiple layers, no suggestive material (not even satire), no glitter, no string or ribbon, no added decorations, no perfume.[79]

---

79   https://web.connectnetwork.com/things-to-send-inmates/

Experience Counts

Inmates of the Eastern New York Correctional Facility in Na-panoch, NY, have become champion debaters. The debate team has out-argued teams from the University of Vermont, West Point, and Harvard.

The inmate team of three is handicapped with difficulties researching. They have no access to the internet, and written materials need to go through a lengthy approval and inspection process. The prison library doesn't have much to offer.

But the team has a big advantage in experience. They are generally older than the college students, and they've seen a side of life far removed from that of middle- and upper-class students. While facts are essential in a debater's arsenal, subjective experience can also be used.

In the debate with Harvard, the ENYCF team was put in the uncomfortable position of defending the denial of education for undocumented immigrant children. Though personally disagreeing with any denial of education, they made the case that such children, being poor, would go to schools so bad they weren't worth attending.[80]

---

80 Lauren Gambino, "Harvard's Prestigious debate team loses to New York prison inmates," The Guardian, Oct. 7, 2015.

Glenn Alan Cheney

Education vs. Incarceration

In 2015, according to the National Association of State Budget Officers, corrections expenditures for state prisons totaled $56.9 billion, an average of more than a billion dollars per state.

In that year, Louisiana had the highest rate of incarceration—776 prisoners per 100,000 residents. Oklahoma followed close behind, followed by Alabama, Mississippi, Arizona, Arkansas and Texas. Four of those seven states were among the ten states with lowest per-pupil spending on education. Maine had the lowest rate of incarceration, 132 per 100,000, followed by Massachusetts, Minnesota, Rhode Island, Vermont, Utah and New Hampshire. Four of those seven states were among the ten states with the highest per-pupil spending on education, though Utah ranked absolute last in per-pupil spending.[81]

---

81 The Sentencing Project citing U.S. Bureau of Justice Statistics for 2015, and governing.com, citing U.S. Census Bureau 2014 Annual Survey of School System Finances. http://www.governing.com/topics/education/gov-education-funding-states.html

Collateral Punishment

War has its "collateral damage." Imprisonment has its "collateral punishment." According to The Sentencing Project:

• One in 50 children in America has a parent in prison.

• In mid-2007, 809,800 of the nation's 1,518,535 state and federal prisoners were parents of children under the age of 18. Of these parents, 65,600 were mothers.

• Fewer than half the parents were living with their children when they were arrested.

• Incarcerated mothers were three times more likely to have been living in a single-parent household than in a two-parent household. Percentage was about the same for fathers.

• Parents in *federal* prison were more likely to have had two-parent households, but mothers were two and a half times more likely to be in a single-parent household.

• About half of the parents in state prisons were their families' primary financial support.

• Nine percent of parents reported homelessness in the year before arrest.

• Mothers were twice as likely to have been homeless.

• Twenty percent of the mothers had a history of physical or sexual abuse.

• Forty-one percent reported a current health problem.

• The prisoners reported having 1,706,600 children, which would be about 2.3 percent of the nation's children.

• Black children were seven and a half times more likely to have a parent in prison.

• Four out of five fathers were black. Five out of ten mothers were white.

• The number of children with a mother in prison increased 131 percent from 1991 to 2007. The number with fathers in prison increased 77 percent. The difference in increase was due to a relative increase in the number of women in prison, up 122 percent.

• About a quarter of the children were under the age of four. A third were under nine. A third would reach the age of 18 before a parent was released from prison.

• Youth whose parents were imprisoned are nearly five times more likely to be imprisoned than children separated from parents for other reasons.[82]

---

82   J. Murray and D.P. Farrington, "The Effects of Parental Imprisonment on Children," Crime and Justice, 2008.

Feasible Reforms

In 2018, Prison Policy Initiative pursued several prison reforms that might make America and various states better places to live.[83]

End Prison Gerrymandering

State governments divide their states into congressional districts according to populations in each district. Some municipalities do the same to allot city council seats. Many states count prisoners as residents wherever they are incarcerated. Thus prisoners count as constituents even though they can't vote. Since a prison houses a large number of people, a district with a prison effectively gives a relatively small number of voters much more political influence. Counting prisoners at their home address would result in more equitable political power. It would also more accurately represent the needs of neighborhoods.

---

83   "Winnable Criminal Justice Reforms," Prison Policy Initiative briefing on promising state reform issues for 2018, https://www.prisonpolicy.org/reports/winnable2018.pdf

Glenn Alan Cheney

Lower the cost of calls home

Why do calls from prisons often cost more than $1.50 per minute? There is no good reason, and communication between inmate and family would help keep families intact and children less traumatized.

Not letting video calls replace in-person visits

Video calls cost prison systems less than in-person visits, but obviously the impact on families is less positive. The money saved isn't worth the social repercussions.

Allowing letters from home in local jails

Incredibly, sheriffs in 14 states are experimenting with a policy of not allowing prisoners to receive letters from home—a dehumanization of an already dehumanizing situation.

Reducing Pretrial Detention

Many prisoners are held simply because they can't afford bail. One result: more plea bargaining, which results in overcrowding, loss of job, apartment, child custody, and higher costs to taxpayers. There are many alternatives to the detention of people not proven guilty.

The Value of Visits

The Minnesota Dept. of Corrections tracked recidivism among 16,420 offenders who were released between 2003 and 2007. It was looking for a relationship between visits in prison and the likelihood of returning to prison. The study found that inmates who were visited had a 13 percent lower risk of recidivism for felony violations and 25 percent for technical violations. Each visit reduced the risk by 0.1 percent. One visit a month reduced it by 0.9 percent. Prisoners visited close to their release date had a 3.6 percent reduction. With each different individual visitor, the risk rate dropped three percent. Visits by siblings, in-laws, fathers, and clergy all had a positive effect. But one visitor had a negative effect: ex-wives.[84]

---

84   "Effects of Prison Visitation on Offender Recidivism," MN Dept. of Corrections, Nov. 2011.

Glenn Alan Cheney

Yet Another Bad Idea

Despite the beneficial effects of visits to prisoners, many prisons are trying to replace them with video visits. Prison administrations say video visits improve safety and reduce the cost of having staff arrange prisoners, check in visitors, and oversee visits. Often video and telecom equipment providers will install video systems for free so that they can collect usage fees from families and prisoners. At least one contract between a provider and a facility required that nonprofessional in-person visits be totally banned. In some cases, the prisons benefit from the fees. South Dakota's Minnehaha County Jail reaped $109,400 in video visiting fees in a two-year period.

A study by the Dept. of Justice listed several limitations of video visits. Many of the limitations relate to the poverty that tends to parallel crime and imprisonment.

- Families may lack computers for remote visits.
- Video systems are often of poor audio and video quality.
- The technology may be confusing the families and inmates.
- Illiteracy can hinder setting up a video visiting account.
- Families are less likely to go to a facility if they cannot have

an in-person visit.

• Fee charged for video visits may be onerous or impossible for poor families.

• Poor families may not have a necessary credit card.

The study said, "Video visiting cannot replicate seeing someone in-person, and it is critical for a young child to visit his or her incarcerated parent in person to establish a secure attachment."[85]

The study quoted a family member saying, "We want to see him for real. We want to touch our hands through the window. It makes him feel better. Even just to kiss the window, it makes us feel better."

---

85   "Video Visiting in Corrections: Benefits, Limitations, and Implementation Considerations," U.S. Dept. of Justice and National Institute of Corrections, Dec. 2014

Glenn Alan Cheney

Rikers

Rikers Island serves as the main jail of the City of New York. Though considered a jail because it's used mostly for short, in-transit stays, by many measures it is larger than most of the world's prisons. Some of the space is actually an asylum for the mentally ill who must be isolated from society.

• The area of the island is 413 acres—four times larger than the original island.

• Ten of New York's 15 corrections facilities are on the island. One of the ten is for women.

• The annual budget is $860 million.

• Staff is larger than many towns, with 9,000 officers and 1,500 other staff.

• Daytime population—staff+inmates—is three times that of Montpelier, VT.

• The facility includes schools, medical clinics, ball fields, chapels, gyms, drug rehab programs, grocery stores, barbershops, a bakery, laundromat, power plant, track, tailor shop, print shop, bus depot, car wash, and a composting plant.

• Inmate capacity is 15,000. Population in 1991 was 21,688.

• 100,000 people are admitted each year, though 90 percent are soon released or transferred.

• The consistent inmate population is about 10,000, most of whom will be released within a year.

• Only 15 percent have been convicted of a crime. The rest are waiting for bail or trial.

• It has been ranked as one of the worst jails or prisons in the United States.

• In 2015, there were 9,424 assaults reported.

• Lawsuits over illegal strip searches at Rikers have cost New York City over $100 million

• 48 percent of adolescents held at Rikers have been diagnosed with mental health issues.

• In 2012, over 14 percent of adolescents were subjected to solitary confinement for an average of 43 days.[86]

---

86   Rikers Island, accessed Jan. 19, 2018, Wikipedia.

Glenn Alan Cheney

Four Consecutive Prison Terms

Prison hulk—a ship no longer capable of going to sea, converted to use as a prison. As a verb, *to hulk* means to convert a ship to a prison.

Oubliette—a dungeon accessible only from a hatchway in a high ceiling. In some cases the hatch is a trapdoor. Oubliette comes from a French word, *oublier*, which means "forget."

Immurement—imprisonment in a walled-in space with no exits and therefore no hope. Also, in most cases, no food or water, making the practice a combination of imprisonment, torture, and execution. The word comes from Latin, *im*, meaning "in" and *murus*, meaning "wall." Edgar Allan Poe's "The Cask of Amontillado" was about an immurement.

Ergastulum—a prison workhouse in ancient Rome, usually underground, where slaves were chained to work as punishment.

Incarceration College

In 2009, a select group of prisoners at Connecticut's high-security Cheshire Correctional Institution were taking courses offered by the elite Wesleyan University. The 19 students earned their seats through a rigorous application process. Among them were six murderers, two drug dealers, and a kidnapper. Collectively, the 19 expected to serve more than 600 years behind bars, and several had little hope of ever taking their education outside the prison.

The students were motivated by the alternative of losing their place in the classes. The courses were of the same content and standards as the ones taught on the university campus. Admission to Wesleyan is extremely competitive. Tuition, room, and board at the time was $51,000 a year. The program was funded for two years by Bard College's Bard Prison Initiative, but future funding was uncertain. Many people complained that the funds might have been better spent helping victims.

The university was named after John Wesley, an 18th century minister who advocated for prison reform. The program was started by two students who had volunteered in prisons and saw the potential.[87]

---

87   Alison Leigh Cowan, "Shoots of College Ivy Sprout at Prison," New York Times, Nov. 17, 2009.

Glenn Alan Cheney

Pay-to-Stay

C riminals in California often have the option to upgrade their cell
for as little as $25 a night in La Verne or as much as $251 a
night in Hermosa Beach. In Monterey Park, $51 will let you serve
your time in half-day increments or just on weekends. Upgraded
cells may include such frills as single occupancy, computer, refrig-
erator, phone, television, and other amenities. The upgrade option
is especially attractive to sexual offenders who would be dangerous-
ly vulnerable among the general prison population. The majority of
upgraders were convicted of traffic offenses, such as DUI, but three
percent of cases were cases that involved violence or sex crimes.
Some of the prisoners come in from other states in order to enjoy
the better conditions. The average cost of a stay is $1,756, but some
prisoners can afford to spend tens of thousands of dollars for a long
sentence. The upgrade option is always at the discretion of a judge.

So if you must commit a crime, make sure it yields enough to
afford decent prison conditions.[88]

---

88   Alysia Santo et al, "Upgrade Your jail cell - for a price," Los Angeles Times,
March 9, 2017 latimes.com/projects/la-me-pay-to-stay-jails/

Does Parole Work?

When New York City decided in 2017 to close its infamous Rikers Island jail complex, the city began releasing as many prisoners as possible. The population of the city's jails fell below 9,000 for the first time in 35 years. At the same time, crime, which had been decreasing, continued to decrease. Just one type of crime rose: parole violations.

New York State was having the same experience. Commitments to prison declined by an amazing 31 percent from 1999 to 2017. Thirteen prisons closed and 6,000 beds were eliminated. The state has been saving $160 million per year. At the same time, the crime rate declined, but re-incarceration for parole violations increased by 21 percent. In 2015, 47 percent of exits from parole were exits into prison for parole violations.

What's interesting is that only 16.3 percent of the recidivism was for crimes other than parole violations. The rest were posing no threat to society.

So one question is, how much could recidivism be reduced by reducing the terms and the length of parole?

And another question is, if recidivism and the monitoring of parole were reduced, might the money saved be better applied to preventing that 16.3 percent from returning to crime?[89]

---

89   Research Brief: "Less is More in New York: An Examination of the Impact of State Parole Violations on Prison and Jail Populations, Columbia University/ Justice Lab, January 29, 2018.

Glenn Alan Cheney

Justice Is Sweeter Than Revenge

Here's an idea: Instead of using prisons as places of punishment, why not use them as places to repair the harm of crime, bring criminal and victim together, and transform people and communities for the better?

Why not give it a shot? We know that the current use of prisons isn't working. Once released, former prisoners tend to return to the life of crime. The deterrent effect isn't very effective. The term "correction" is generally a joke.

The concept of Restorative Justice offers a different way to use and perhaps avoid or minimize the use of prisons. Rather than focus on counter-productive punishment, it focuses on repairing the harm done by crime. It brings together all stakeholders—offender, victim, and community. It makes amends possible. It assuages victims by inducing offenders to take responsibility for their actions. It helps offenders become safe, constructive members of their community.

The four cornerstones of restorative justice are:

1. Inclusion of all parties,

2. Encountering the other side,

3. Making amends for the harm,

4. Reintegration of all parties to their communities.

Ten Commandments of Restorative Justice

I.   You will focus on the harm of crime rather than the rules that have been broken,

II. You will be equally concerned about victims and offenders, involving both in the process of justice,

III. You will work toward the restoration of victims, empowering them and responding to their needs as they see them,

IV. You will support offenders while encouraging them to understand, accept, and carry out their obligations,

V.   You will recognize that while obligations may be difficult for offenders, they should not be intended as pain,

VI. You will provide opportunities for dialogue, direct or indirect, between victim and offender as appropriate,

VII. You will find meaningful ways to involve the community and to respond to the community bases of crime,

VIII. You will encourage collaboration and reintegration rather than coercion and isolation,

IX. You will be mindful of the unintended consequences of your actions and programs,

X.   You will show respect to all parties—victims, offenders, justice colleagues.[90]

---

90   restorativejustice.org

For the Well Appointed Prison

Part of the prison-industrial complex is the companies that supply "detention equipment"—everything from disposable handcuffs to soccer balls. You can get "virtually indestructible" padded cells and padded cell repair kits. You can get a ready-made entry guard tower. You can get anti-shank razors, jumpsuits in orange or stripes, dental floss, belly chains, coffee mugs, humane body wrap, suicide safety blankets, economy bath towels, stainless interviewing chair, miniature "DOC" tactical vest beverage holder, "gotcha" tamper-proof handcuffs, rappelling gloves, *CO's Guide to Understanding Inmates*, a full riot suit, correctional officer wife charm bracelet, exam gloves, "My Heart Belongs to a Correctional Officer" sweater, and CrossBar brand electronic cigarettes.[91]

---

91 bobbarker.com, anchortex.com, americandetentionsupplies.com, icswaco.com, correctionsone.com, aspiregear.com

Cashless Prisons

In Belgium, the "Prison Cloud" program introduced in 2015 is now running in three prisons, involving a cloud-based digital service enabling prisoners to purchase items, watch video on demand, make phone calls and access limited pages on the internet, for example. The Prison Cloud also allows for a centralized electronic file for every prisoner that can be used by all relevant agencies, including medical files. Cashless prisons can be found in many countries from Georgia, to Thailand and Finland.[92]

---

92   Eeva Haaramo, "Inmates in Finland's prisons no longer need to use cash as a pre-paid card system is rolled out," ComputerWeekly.com, June 28, 2016.

Glenn Alan Cheney

Women and Children

Why Women Go to Prison

The female prison population has been rising all over the world. While the total number of prisoners has risen 20 percent since 2000, the number of female prisoners has risen by 50 percent. The estimate in 2015 was about 700,000 women and girls being held in 219 national prison systems.

What have women been doing wrong? According to a report from Penal Reform International, a "high number" were charged with or convicted of nonviolent minor offenses generally relating to poverty and "family roles," including property and drug-related offenses.[93]

A 2016 study in Kenya, for example, found that, of 97 women interviewed, 36 percent were being held for illegally brewing and selling alcohol.[94]

In 2014, 80 percent of female prisoners in Ireland had been convicted of nothing more serious than not paying fines.[95]

---

93   Global Prison Trends 2017, London, UK, penalreform.org

94   Roy Walmsley, World Female Imprisonment List (third edition), Institute for Criminal Policy Research, 2015.

95   Fiona Gartland, "Non-payment of fines reason for 80% of female committals," The Irish Times, 27 June 2016, www. irishtimes.com/news/crime-and-law/non- payment-of-fines-reason-for-80-of-female- committals-1.2701713.

In England and Wales, 36 percent of women in prison were locked up for not paying a mandatory "television license" fee.[96]

In Sierra Leone, the rate of arrest for women was attributed to the Ebola epidemic, when women were selling goods and food during curfew hours or gathering crowds after a family member had died.

In 2016, over 90 percent of women in prison in Indonesia and Philippines were charged with drug-related offenses. In Thailand in 2013, 83 percent were under similar charges. In Cambodia, many women arrested for drug offenses had been coerced into the crime by their male partners.[97]

In Argentina, Brazil, Costa Rica, and Peru, 60 percent of women prisoners were charged with drug offenses.[98]

The United Nations General Assembly Session on drugs recognized the special vulnerabilities of women and called on nations to address protective and risk factors.

---

96   Prison Reform Trust, Why focus on reducing women's imprisonment?, February 2017, p2. A 'television licence' is required by law to install or use a TV or watch programmes on an online TV service.

97   Chontit Chuenurah and Min Jee Yamada Park, Women Prisoners in Southeast Asia: Their Profiles and Pathways to Prison, Korean Journal of Correctional Discourse, submitted in December 2016.

98   www.wola.org/women-drug-policies-and-incarceration-in-the-americas/.

White Women Rising Downward

In the United States in June 2016. African-Americans were imprisoned at more than five times the rate of whites. In five states, the rate was ten times higher.[99]

But the rate was different for female inmates, data from 2015 indicates that the number of imprisoned black women was declining while that of white women increased. Still, in 2014, the rate of imprisonment of black women was more than double that of white women, 109 per 100,000 versus 53. The national average was 65 out of 100,000 women, with wide variation among states. Oklahoma led with 1,423 per, with Rhode Island last at 12. The overall rate of imprisonment increased 50 percent faster for women and than for men between 2000 and 2014. In 2014, 106,232 women were in prison, 109,100 were in jail, 102,825 were on parole, and 966,029 were on probation, a total of about 1.2 million.[100]

99   "Fact Sheet: Incarcerated Women and Girls," The Sentencing Project, 2015.

100   Ashley Nellis, "The Color of Justice: Racial and Ethnic Disparity in State Prisons," The Sentencing Project, June 2016.

Glenn Alan Cheney

Girls (under 18 years of age) were behind bars for "status offenses and technical violations" far more often than boys. These are
offenses such as truancy and running away—violations that would
not apply to adults. Thirty-four percent of girls were in for such violations, compared with 20 percent of boys. Boys were more likely
arrested for crimes involving persons, property, or public order. Boys
and girls were about equal for drug offenses, which was the least
common offense.

International Law on
Imprisonment of Children

How many children (people under 18) are in prison? Nobody knows. Many countries don't count them, and it depends on the definition of "prison." Just as a prison for adults may be euphemized as a "correctional facility," prisons for children are known by such softer terms "detention center" or "young offenders institution."

UNICEF estimates a round number of 1,000,000 around the world. In many cases—again, no one knows how many—prison conditions are decrepit and abusive, with no possibility of education or rehabilitation.

As with the imprisonment of adults, the United States leads the world. In 2011, 60,000 children were imprisoned in juvenile detention centers. Another 95,000 were locked in adult prisons.

Often the children are imprisoned for offenses that would not be crimes if committed by adults. In Texas in 2010, Texas imprisoned over 6,000 children for such "status offenses" as truancy, underage drinking, running away from home, and curfew violations.

In Saudi Arabia, girls (and adult women) can imprisoned and flogged for such crimes as "seclusion" and "mingling," which include "being in a apartment by herself...or sitting in a place where she is not natural for her to be."

In Israel, children as young as 11 have been arrested, choked, beaten, threatened, and interrogated without parents or lawyers present. They are automatically prosecuted and sentenced by military courts.

Juvenile offenders have been put on death row in Egypt, Iran, Maldives, Pakistan, Saudi Arabia, Sri Lanka, Sudan, Yemen, and Nigeria. Children in 73 countries, including the United States, can receive death sentences.[101]

---

101 "Children Behind Bars: The Global Overuse of Detention of Children," Human Rights Watch, 2016.

53,000

On any given day, 53,000 youths are held in some kind of prison. Nearly one in ten is in an adult jail or prison. Of the 48,000 in juvenile facilities, 31 percent are no older than 15. More than 500 are under the age of 12.

Here are nine types of juvenile facilities:

Correctional Facilities

1. Detention Center: Temporary restriction pending court disposition or awaiting placement elsewhere.

2. Long-term secure Facility: Strict confinement but with training, schools, reformatories.

3. Reception/Diagnostic Center: Short-term facility pending assignment to another facility.

Residential

4. Treatment Center: Facility focused on individual treatment for drug abuse, sex offense, mental health, etc.

5 Group Home: Long-term facility where residents are allowed contact with community, school attendance, job, etc.

6. Ranch/Wilderness Camp: Long-term facility for youth who do not need confinement, with activities on ranch, farm, forestry camp,

etc.

7. Shelter: Short-term facility with little physical restriction, typically for runaways and homeless youth.

8. Boot Camp: Secure facility with military-style physical and mental training, with strict rules and drilling to break youth resistance to improvement and cooperation.

9. Other: Alternative schools, independent living, etc.

In 2015, at least 30,714 youths were held in detention centers, long-term secure facilities, or reception centers. Two out of three were held in the most restrictive facilities—the juvenile equivalent of jails and prisons, 4,656 of them in facilities for adults.

Over 4,000 of those in detention centers were there for low-level "technical violations" or "status offenses such" as probation violations, which are not considered law violations for adults. Almost half of all youths held for status offenses are locked up for over 90 days.

The Prison Policy Initiative (which provided all the above information) calculates that one in three youths under detention—17,000 people—could be released without endangering the public. Another 6,000 are being held without being tried or found guilty of delinquent.[102]

---

102   Wendy Sawyer, "Youth Confinement: The Whole Pie," Prison Policy Initiative news release, Feb. 27, 2018.

Mothers' Duress

The Great American Incarceration[103] that began in the 1980s landed a lot of mothers in prison—65,000 of them by 2010. Because of women's traditional importance to family life and household health, the imprisonment of a mother impacts society in several ways. Children end up with alternative caregivers, often landing in different families, schools, and towns. Households often lose a wage earner. Life at home often deteriorates as the father (if any) attempts to hold a job while taking care of everything from laundry to help with homework.

The impact on the mothers themselves is also especially serious, and white women suffer even more. Researchers refer to "spoiled identity" as mothers suffer the stigma of failing to fulfill the classic function of a mother—to nurture her children. Fathers are impacted in the same way, but generally not as severely. All incarcerated parents have to grapple with the reality of no longer being primarily a parent. Rather, most of their time is dedicated to being an inmate.

White women suffer more for several reasons, each in a way resulting from an easier life prior to imprisonment.

---

103   Beth A. Eaterling and Ben Feldermeyer, "Race, Incarceration, and Motherhood: Spoiled Identity among Rural White Mothers in Prison," *The Prison Journal*, March 2017.

• Since Hispanic and black women tend to live in families more beset by problems relating to prejudice and poverty, their wider families are more prepared psychologically to take on the burden of a family member's children. White families tend to take on that burden, but they are more upset about it.

• Since a higher proportion of black women end up incarcerated, they aren't quite as shocked to find themselves behind bars. Shocked, yes, of course, but not as shocked by "how far they've fallen."

• As above, white communities tend to stigmatize the arrest of a community member more than black communities do. Whites may see the arrest as disgrace, while blacks may see it as injustice.

• The nature of their respective crimes tends to land black women in prisons closer to home than white women. Consequently, the black women maintain closer contact with families.

• Blacks, especially those in poor urban communities, often grow up in a kind of isolation from general society, a situation somewhat similar to that of prison. Whites grow up in relative social acceptance, increasing the shock upon imprisonment.

Ironically, the greater degree of suffering for white mother prisoners results from their relatively wealthier and easier pre-prison lives.

When Mothers Get Locked Up

In 2009, nearly five percent of children in the United States knew what it was like to have a mother in prison. A study found an increasing rate of "at-risk familial environments" such as drug abuse, violence, etc., resulting from maternal incarceration.[104] Seventy percent of imprisoned mothers reported physical or sexual abuse prior to arrest, and two-thirds of those said the abuse occurred while they were living with their children.

Separation from a mother due to incarceration may be the most damaging aspect of incarceration. Children with incarcerated mothers

• have higher rates of externalizing emotions through aggression, problem behaviors, and delinquency;

• have higher rates of internalizing emotions resulting in depression, fearfulness, sleep problems, and low self-esteem;

• have higher levels of anxiety;

• are more likely to hang out with "negative peers";

104   Zina T. McGree, Bertha L. Davis, Tyrell Connor, Samaria Haysbert, Alfreada B. Kelly, "Examining the Relationship between Children's Behavioral Outcomes and Life Events among Incarcerated Mothers," Journal of Social Welfare and Human Rights, Dec. 2014.

- report long-term trauma due to separation from their mothers;
- are more likely to suffer emotional detachment from substitute caregivers;
- often show symptoms of post-traumatic stress disorder, among them flashbacks and feelings of anger and guilt;
- more likely to suffer poverty upon their mother's release from prison;
- often feel anger at their mother.

Born Behind Bars

In 2016 a woman was forced to give birth on the floor of a cell in the Macomb County (Michigan) Jail. Arrested for driving with a suspended license. Unable to pay a $10,000 cash bond, she was being held five days until a court date. She informed officials that she was eight months pregnant. When she told jail staff that she was going into labor, they did not believe her. They refused to take her to a hospital. When it became undeniable that she was about to have a baby, jail medical staff tried to help, but the mother-to-be was kept in her cell. She gave birth on a thin mattress on the floor. The medical staff had never delivered a baby before. The baby weighed less than five pounds but survived.[105]

---

105   Mark Hicks, "Macomb County Jail birth sparks controversy," The Detroit News, Feb. 7, 2017.

Glenn Alan Cheney

Babies in the Hoosgow

Nearly 100 countries, from South Sudan to France, have laws
that allow incarcerated mothers to stay with their newborn babies. The United States is not one of them. Only eight of more than
100 U.S. prisons for women have nursery facilities for babies born
while their mothers are serving time. There used to be more, but with
the advent of mass incarceration and get-tough-on-crime legislation,
there has been less room, less financial support, and an increased
belief that letting a mother be with her newborn was not consistent
with the spirit of punishment.

Of the eight still in operation, Bedford Hills Correctional Facility has the oldest prison nursery in the country, operating since
1901. The walls and rooms of the nursery look like those of any good
nursery school, full of colors, images, and toys. The big difference
is the bars on the windows, the armed guards, the razor wire on the
walls outside.

Babies at Bedford can spend their first 18 months with their mothers. Recidivism among these mothers is about 13 percent, half of the 26 percent rate for Bedford inmates as a whole.

The other states with incarceration nurseries are Indiana, Ohio, Nebraska, South Dakota, Washington, and West Virginia. Eighteen months is the typical time allowed, and generally restrictions don't allow participation by women arrested for violence or child abuse.[106]

---

106 Darren Boyle, "Raised behind bars: Inside America's maximum security prisons where babies get to stay with their felon mothers while they serve their mail sentences," The Daily Mail (online) May 25, 2016. http://www.dailymail.co.uk/news/article-3608322/Born-bars-Inside-America-s-maximum-security-prisons-babies-stay-felon-mothers-serve-jail-sentences.html

Glenn Alan Cheney

Labor in Chains

Roughly six percent of female prisoners—some 200,000 women—were pregnant when they were incarcerated. There is no accurate number of how many prisoners in the United States give birth each year. The estimate is about 2,000.

Shackling pregnant prisoners while they are in labor is legal in about half the country, and it's often practiced even where illegal. It has been illegal in federal prisons since 2008.

Illinois was the first state to pass a law prohibiting the shackling of female prisoners while they are giving birth. Thirteen years later, 80 women claimed to have been in shackles while in labor.

New York passed such a law in 2009, but in 2015, 23 of 27 women who gave birth while incarcerated said they'd been in shackled during labor. In 2011, Tina Tinen, at Bedford Hills Correctional Facility, was shackled while taken to the hospital and until 15 minutes of giving birth. In 2012, another prisoner there, Jacqueline McDougall, was handcuffed to a chain around her waist, clamped at the sutured incision where she'd had a C-section.[107]

Pennsylvania allows shackles during childbirth. From July 2012 to June 2013, over 100 women gave birth while in shackles.

In 2011, Valerie Nabors, in jail for stealing casino chips, was shack-

---

107   Audrey Quinn, "In Labor, in Chains," New York Times, July 26, 2014

led in an ambulance and during childbirth despite repeated requests by medical staff to remove the restraints. She was released during the moments of birth but re-shackled ten minutes later. The incident occurred 18 days after restraint of pregnant patients was made illegal. She was later unable to receive physical therapy because guards refused to unshackle her ankles.[108]

April, 2013, Melissa Hall, 25, a prisoner at Milwaukee County Jail, is shackled—right wrist, left ankle—while in labor at a hospital for three hours. She remained shackled for the next two days.[109]

Shawanna Nelson was six months pregnant when she was given a short sentence in an Arkansas prison for a nonviolent crime. When she went into labor, her ankles were shackled on opposite sides of her bed until she was taken to the delivery room. She was re-shackled immediately following the birth.

In 2017 a jury awarded an anonymous woman $6.7 million after she accused a Milwaukee County Jail guard of raping her several times, including right before childbirth. She was shackled while giving birth and days afterward. The guard pleaded guilty to lesser charges and was sentenced to three days in jail and a fine of $200.[110]

---

108   Sean Whaley, "$130,000 settlement eyed for a pregnant inmate who was shackled," Las Vegas Review-Journal, Nov. 29, 2013.

109   Rebecca Nelson, *Cosmopolitan*, October 25, 2017.

110   John Diedrich, "Jury awards $6.7 million to inmate raped by guard in Milwaukee County Jail, shackled during childbirth," Milwaukee Journal Sentinel, June 7, 2017.

There Are No Words for Such a Birth

Tianna Laboy was 19 years old and pregnant for the first time while incarcerated at York Correctional Institution in Niantic, Conn. On February 9, 2018 she reported a clear discharge from her vagina and a feelingof mild abdominal discomfort. Her belly dropped, and she experiemced excruciating back pain. She was told she couldn't see medical staff because she hadn't filled out the proper paperwork. After filling the paperwork out, she was told that OB/GYN services were not available that day.

Two days later, her discharge was thicker and bloody. Health workers told her to go back to her cell until contractions were two minutes apart. By February 12, she felt her stomach was "twisting inside out." She called for medical help but was only given a glass of water and a heating pad. She cried out in pain all night. Guards checked on her regularly but told her that medical staff refused to see her.

By 4:30 a.m., she reported a large amount of bloody discharge. With no femin inme hygiene products available, she staggered to breakfast with a T-shirt stuffed between her legs, then staggered back to her cell, leaning against walls all the way. At 6:30, she thought she had to go to the bathroom. She was seated on the toilet in her cell when she realized the baby was crowning. The newborn emerged quickly, falling into the toilet. Se she bumped her head as she fell into the water. Tianna and her cellmate pulled the girl from the water and patted her on the back to get the fluid out. Then the baby began to breathe. Mother and child were then transported to a hospital.

The Connecticut Department of Corrections investigated. A year later, it had not reached a conclusion. Laboy sued the DOC for deliberate indifference, negligence, and false imprisonment. The latter charge referred, of course, to the infant.[111]

---

111   Jenna Carlesso, The Connecticut Mirror, March 5, 2019.

Glenn Alan Cheney

Illegitimate Births

A report on the treatment of pregnant or postpartum women by
The Prison Birth Project and Prisoners' Legal Services of Massachusetts found that

- neither the state Department of Corrections nor any single
Country Sheriff's Office fully complied with the law;

- corrections staff showed varying knowledge of the law;

- women were being illegally restrained without reason after giving birth;

- pregnant women had been illegally transported in vans with
no seatbelts;

- pregnant women were illegally denied sufficiently nutritious
meals, and often they went hungry;

- pregnant women were given standard-issue clothing with pant
legs so long they could cause the women to trip;

- prisoners who had delivered by cesarean section were illegally
restrained by waist chains during transportation shortly after giving
birth.

A woman who was handcuffed during labor said, "It was really hard. I couldn't move like I needed to—couldn't hold my stomach or push up to move myself around. The metal would dig into me every time I did try to grab my stomach during a contraction. It was incredibly lonely going through that experience by myself."[112]

---

112   Rachel Roth, Lauren Petit, Marianne Bullock, "Breaking Promises: Violations of the Massachusetts Pregnancy Standards & Anti-shackling Law," Prisoners' Legal Services of Massachusetts and The Prison Birth Project. May 2016.

Glenn Alan Cheney

Words of Wisdom

To live in prison is to live without mirrors. To live without mirrors is to live without the self.

Margaret Atwood

No prison can shut out God.

J.F. La Harpe

Is it surprising that prisons resemble factories, schools, barracks, hospitals, which all resemble prisons?

Michel Foucault

Jails and state prisons are the complement of schools: so many less as you have of the latter, so many more must you have of the former.

Horace Mann

How feeble is all language to describe the horrors we inflict upon these wretches, whom we mason up in the cells of our prisons, and condemn to perpetual solitude in the very heart of our population.

Herman Melville

It is in prison...that one becomes a real revolutionary.

Vladimir Lenin

Glenn Alan Cheney

Prison is like high school with knives.

Raegan Butcher

Show me a prison, show me a jail
Show me a pris'ner whose face has grown pale
And I'll show you a young man
With many reasons why
There but for fortune, go you or I.

Phil Ochs

While there is a lower class, I am in it, and while there is a criminal element, I am of it, and while there is a soul in prison, I am not free.

Eugene V. Debs

Some prisons don't require bars to keep people locked inside. All it takes is their perception that they belong there.

Lysa TerKeurst

At the risk of quoting Mephistopheles I repeat: Welcome to hell. A hell erected and maintained by human-governments, and blessed by black robed judges. A hell that allows you to see your loved ones, but not to touch them. A hell situated in America's boondocks, hundreds of miles away from most families. A white, rural hell, where most of the captives are black and urban. It is an American way of death.

Mumia Abu-Jamal

If they lock me up, at least I'll have a place to stay.

Mike Tyson

A prison is ... a microcosm, a little world of woe, it is a map of misery, it is a place that will learn a young man more villainy, if he be apt to take it, in one half year, than he can learn at twenty dicing-houses, bowling alleys, brothel houses, or ordinaries; and an old man, more policy than if he had been pupil to Machiavelli.

Geffray Minshull

"No one truly knows a nation until one has been inside its jails. A nation should not be judged by how it treats its highest citizens but its lowest ones."

Nelson Mandela

America is a land of the second chance—and when the gates of the prison open, the path ahead should lead to a better life.

George W. Bush

You can tell a lot about a civilization by the quality of the people found in its jails.

David Gerrold

He who opens a school door closes a prison.

Victor Hugo

"Remember those in prison as if you were their fellow prisoners, and those who are mistreated as if you yourselves were suffering.

Hebrews 13:3

138

It must surely be a tribute to the resilience of the human spirit that even a small number of those men and women in the hell of the prison system survive it and hold on to their humanity.

Howard Zinn

Poor people, people of color especially, are much more likely to be found in prison than in institutions of higher education.

Angela Davis

The last place I would ever want to go is prison.

Martha Stewart

The only time you can be completely free from risk is when you're in prison.

Edward Snowden

Year after year the gates of prison hells return to the world an emaciated, deformed, will-less, ship-wrecked crew of humanity, with the Cain mark on their foreheads, their hopes crushed, all their natural inclinations thwarted. With nothing but hunger and inhumanity to greet them, these victims soon sink back into crime as the only possibility of existence. It is not at all an unusual thing to find men and women who have spent half their lives—nay, almost their entire existence—in prison.

Emma Goldman

Prison is a second-by-second assault on the soul, a day-to-day degradation of the self, an oppressive steel and brick umbrella that transforms seconds into hours and hours into days.

Mumia Abu-Jamal

The best way to keep a prisoner from escaping is to make sure he never knows he is in prison.

Fyodor Dostoevsky

Your definition of who you are is your prison. You can set yourself free at any time.

Cheri Huber

Security without liberty is called prison

Benjamin Franklin

I think the years I have spent in prison have been the most formative and important in my life because of the discipline, the sensations, but chiefly the opportunity to think clearly, to try to understand things.

Jawaharlal Nehru

I think my attitude to human beings has changed since leaving prison.

Jeffrey Archer

Glenn Alan Cheney

There is no glory in punishing.

Michel Foucault

Why should they ask me to put on a uniform and go 10,000 miles from home and drop bombs and bullets on brown people in Vietnam while so-called Negro people in Louisville are treated like dogs and denied simple human rights? No, I'm not going 10,000 miles from home to help murder and burn another poor nation simply to continue the domination of white slave masters of the darker people the world over. This is the day when such evils must come to an end. I have been warned that to take such a stand would cost me millions of dollars. But I have said it once and I will say it again. The real enemy of my people is here. I will not disgrace my religion, my people or myself by becoming a tool to enslave those who are fighting for their own justice, freedom and equality. If I thought the war was going to bring freedom and equality to 22 million of my people they wouldn't have to draft me, I'd join tomorrow. I have nothing to lose by standing up for my beliefs. So I'll go to jail, so what? We've been in jail for 400 years.

Muhammad Ali

The greater ignorance towards a country is not ignoring what its politicians have to say, it is ignoring what the inmates in its prisons have to say.

Criss Jami

He who has never tasted jail
Lives well within the legal pale,
While he who's served a heavy sentence
Renews the racket, not repentance.

Ogden Nash

...the court, as now constituted, would be meaningless without the jail which gives it its power. But if there is anything I have learned by being in jail, it is that prisons are wrong, simply and unqualifiedly wrong.

Barbara Deming

Do not fear ARREST. Why? Because, there is REST at the end of each AR"REST"; either in jail or in the grave. The wisest and the greatest of men are aware of this.

Oppong Amankwaa

It is a sad state of affairs in the USA that for the sick and the poor that jail offers better benefits than the freedom of no healthcare, bills that cannot be paid and starvation.

Steven Magee

[Prison] relieves us of the responsibility of seriously engaging with the problems of our society, especially those produced by racism and, increasingly, global capitalism.

Angela Davis

The least I can do is speak out for the hundreds of chimpanzees who, right now, sit hunched, miserable and without hope, staring out with dead eyes from their metal prisons. They cannot speak for themselves.

Jane Goodall

All these [correctional] institutions seemed purposely invented for the production of depravity and vice, condensed to such a degree that no other conditions could produce it, and for the spreading of this condensed depravity and vice broadcast among the whole population.

Leo Tolstoy

A society with a great number of prisons is a totally failed society because it has terribly failed to create a marvelous society where crime is not something widespread but an exception!

Mehmet Murat Ildan

Under a government which imprisons any unjustly, the true place for a just man is also a prison.

Henry David Thoreau

The most anxious man in a prison is the governor.

George Bernard Shaw

We are all serving a life sentence in the dungeon of the self.

Cyril Connolly

To assert in any case that a man must be absolutely cut off from society because he is absolutely evil amounts to saying that society is absolutely good, and no-one in his right mind will believe this today.

Albert Camus

It isn't true that convicts live like animals: animals have more room to move around.

Mario Vargas Llosa

Prison is a socialist paradise where equality prevails, everything is supplied, and competition is eliminated.

Elbert Hubbard

Being in prison for seven years was like being in an army that never drilled, never deployed, and only fought itself.

Raegan Butcher

Prison is, simply put, the bottom rung of the welfare ladder.

Stephen Reid

Prison is the only form of public housing that the government has truly invested in over the past five decades.

Marc Lamont Hill

Prison is the recruitment center for the army of crime. That is what it achieves.

Michel Foucault

Prison is an expensive way of making bad people worse.

Douglas Hurd

Going to prison is like dying with your eyes open.

Bernard Kerik

Building prisons to fight crime is like building cemeteries to fight disease.

Jack Levin

Mistakes are Made

From Michelle Alexander's *The New Jim Crow: Mass Incarceration in the Age of Colorblindness*:

The genius of the current caste system, and what most distinguishes it from its predecessors, is that it appears voluntary. People choose to commit crimes, and that's why they are locked up or locked out, we are told. This feature makes the politics of responsibility particularly tempting, as it appears the system can be avoided with good behavior. But herein lies the trap. All people make mistakes. All of us are sinners. All of us are criminals. All of us violate the law at some point in our lives. In fact, if the worst thing you have ever done is speed ten miles over the speed limit on the freeway, you have put yourself and others at more risk of harm than someone smoking marijuana in the privacy of his or her living room. Yet there are people in the United States serving life sentences for first-time drug offenses, something virtually unheard of anywhere else in the world."

Suggested Reading

Abbott, Jack Henry. *In the Belly of the Beast* (Vintage, 1991).

Alexander, Buzz. Is William Martinez. *Not Our Brother: Twenty Years of the Prison Creative Arts* (U. of Michigan Press, 2010).

Alexander, Michelle. *The New Jim Crow: Mass Incarceration in the Age of Colorblindnes*s (The New Press, 2010).

Alsner, Alan. *Gates of Injustice: The Crisis in America's Prisons* (FT Press, 2006).

Anderson, Brian. *Inmate to Convict: A Guide to Prison Survival and the Art of Penitentiary Warfare* (Amazon Digital, 2016).

Baca, Jimmy Santiago. *A Place to Stand* (Grove Press, 2002).

Bernstein, Nell. *Burning Down the House: The End of Juvenile Prison* (The New Press, 2016).

Betts, R. Dwayne. *A Question of Freedom: A Memoir of Learning, Survival, and Coming of Age in Prison* (Avery, 2010).

Bonhoffer, Dietrich. *Letters & Papers from Prison* (Touchstone, 1997).

Braly, Malcolm. *On the Yard* (NYRB Classics, 2002).

Casella, Jean, et al, editors. *Hell is a Very Small Place: Voices from Solitary Confinement* (The New Press, 2017).

Clear, Todd R. *Imprisoning Communities: How Mass Incarceration Makes Disadvantaged Neighborhoods Worse* (Oxford U. Press,

2007).

Cleaver, Eldridge, *Soul on Ice* (Delta, 1999).

Conover, Ted. *Newjack: Guarding Sing Sing* (Vintage, 2001).

Davis, Angela Y. *Are Prison's Obsolete?* (Seven Stories Press, 2003).

Davis, Angela Y. *Abolition Democracy: Beyond Empire, Prison, and Torture* (Seven Stories Press, 2005).

Dreisinger, Baz. *Incarceration Nation A Journey to Justice in Prisons Around the World* (Other Press, 2016).

Earley, Pete. *The Hot House: Life Inside Leavenworth Prison* (Bantam, 1993).

Echols, Damien, *Life After Death* (Blue Rider Press, 2012).

Ferguson, Russell. *Prison Survival Guide: Words of Wisdom and Encouragement from an Inmate,* (Rosedog Books, 2016).

Forman, James Jr. *Locking Up Our Own: Crime and Punishment in Black America* (Farrar, Straus and Giroux, 2018).

Foucault, Michel. *Discipline and Punish: The Birth of the Prison* (Pantheon, 1977).

Friedman, Lawrence M. *Crime and Punishment in American History* (HarperCollins, 1993).

Hirsch, Adam J. *The Rise of the Penitentiary: Prisons and Punishment in Early America* (Yale U Press, 1992).

Humes, Edward. *No Matter How Loud I Shout: A Year in the Life of Juvenile Court* (Simon & Schuster, 2015).

Jackson, George. *Soledad Brother* (Chicago Review Press, 1994).

Kudin, Andrew V. How to Survive Prison (Amazon Digital, 2012).

Lamb, Wally. *Couldn't Keep It to Myself: Wally Lamb and the Women of York Correctional Institution* (Harper Perennial, 2004).

Lamb, Wally. *I'll Fly Away: Further Testimonies from the Women of York Prison* (Harper Perennial 2008).

Lerner, Jimmy A. *You Got Nothing Coming: Notes from a Prison Fish* (Broadway, 2002).

Lordan, Christopher, and Dellelo, Robert. *The Factory: A Journey Through the Prison Industrial Complex* (Createspace, 2016).

Loury, Glenn C. et al. *Race, Incarceration, and American Values* (MIT Press, 2008).

Martin, Dannie M., and Sussman, Peter Y. *Committing Journalism: The Prison writings of Red Hog* (W.W. Norton, 1995).

Maur, Marc. *Race to Incarcerate* (New Press, 1999).

McCoy, Kemp. *First Timers Guide on How to Survive in New York State Prison* (Trafford, 2013).

M<cShane, Marilyn D., and Williams, Frank R. *Encyclopedia of American Prisons* (Garland, 1996).

Mitchel, William. *How to Survive Prison for the First Time Inmate: Take a Look at a Dangerous Society within our Society* (Createspace, 2009).

Moran, Brian. *The Justice Impreative: How Hyper-Incarceration Has Hijacked the American Dream* (Malt Justice Initiative, 2014).

Orland, Leonard. Prisons: *Houses of Darkness* (Free Press, 1975).

Osborne, Thomas Mott. *Society and Prisons* (Yale U Press, 1916).

Parenti, Christian. *Lockdown America: Police and Prisons in the Age of Crisis* (Verso, 2008).

Peltier, Leonard. *Prison Writings: My Life is My Sundance* (St. Martin's Griffin, 2000).

Petersilla, Joan. *When Prisoners Come Home: Parole and Prisoner Re-entry* (Oxford U Press, 2003).

Pfaf, John. *Locked In: The True Causes of Mass Incarceration—and How to Achieve True Reform* (Basic Books, 2017).

Rafter, Nicole Hahn, and Stanley, Debra L. *Prisons in America: A Reference Handboo*k (ABC-CLIO, 1999).

Rathbone, Christina. *A World Apart: Women, Prison, and Life Behind Bars* (Random House Trade, 2006).

Reiter, Keramet. 23/7: *Pelican Bay Prison and the Rise of Long-Term Solitary Confinement* (Yale U. Press, 2016).

Prejean, Sr. Helen. *Dead Man Walking* (Vintage, 2011).

Prejean, Sr. Helen. *The Death of Innocents: An Eyewitness Account of Wrongful Execution*s (Vintage, 2006).

Jamonz M. Ross, Jamonz M. and Ross, Taleana K. *How to Do Time: What to Expect and How to Survive When Going to Prison*, (Kindle, 2017).

Ross, Jeffrey Ian. *Behind Bars: Surviving Prison* (Alpha, 2002).

Runnels, Travis. *How to Survive in Prison: A Guide for Prisoners, their Families and Supporters* (Createspace, 2017).

Scaife, Jennifer. *Is It Safe? Essays by Students in the San Quentin College Program* (Prison University Project, 2008).

Santos, Michael G. *Inside: Life Behind Bars in America* (St. Martin's Press, 2007).

Solzhenitsyn, Alexandr, *The Gulag Archipelago 1918-1956: An Experiment in Literary Investigation* (Harper & Row, 1975).

Sykes, G.M. *Society of Captives: A Study of a Maximum Security Prison* (Princeton U. Press, 2007).

Thompson, Heather Ann. *Blood in the Water: The Attica Prison Uprising of 1971 and Its Legacy* (Vintage, 2016).

Thurber, Thomas. *There Are Alternatives to Incarceration: A Study Proposal Written for the Connecticut Prison Association* (Connecticut Prison Assoc, 1973).

Unseem, Bert, and Kimball, Peter, *States of Seige: U.S. Prison Riots 1971-1986* (Oxford U. Press, 2016).

Von Drehle, David. *Among the Lowest of the Dead* (U. of Michigan Press, 2006).

Waldman, Ayelet. *Inside This Place, But Not Of It: Narratives from Women's Prisons* (McSweeny's, 2014).

——, "What Works? Questions and Answers about Prison Reform" (*Public Interest*, Spring 1974).

Yackle, Larry. *Reform and Regre: The Story of Federal Judicial Involvement in the Alabama Prison System* (Oxford U. Press, 1989)

Christopher Zoukis. *Federal Prison Handbook: the Definitive Guide to Surviving the Federal Bureau of Prison* (Middle St. Pub. 2017.

Acknowledgements

The author of this book is really just a hunter-gatherer of information produced by other people and organizations. To see a list of them, just look at the authors of the footnotes. Especially worthy of note are The Sentencing Project and the Prison Policy Initiative. The author also thanks New London Librarium senior editors Denise Dembinski and Ralph Hunter Cheney for their sharp eyes and astute suggestions.

The Author

Glenn Alan Cheney is the author of more than 30 books of fiction and nonfiction, several hundred articles, and a number of stories, poems, op-ed essays, translations, and other works. His books explore such disparate topics as the Pilgrims, Abraham Lincoln, nuns, Brazil's Estrada Real, Brazil's Quilombo dos Palmares, bees, cats, death and burial, imprisonment, nuclear issues, Amazonian Indians, teens with disabilities, drug addiction, Central American issues, Chernobyl, Mohandas Gandhi, and Swaziland. He has translated stories by Machado de Assis and books by Rubem Alves. He is managing editor of New London Librarium. He lives in Hanover, Conn.